29/10/82
3858

£12.80

Library of
Davidson College

ANCIENT JEWISH LAW
Three Inaugural Lectures

ANCIENT JEWISH LAW

Three Inaugural Lectures

BY

DAVID DAUBE

LEIDEN / E. J. BRILL / 1981

ISBN 90 04 06531 8

Copyright 1981 by E. J. Brill, Leiden, The Netherlands

All rights reserved. No part of this book may be reproduced or translated in any form, by print, photoprint, microfilm, microfiche or any other means without written permission from the publisher

PRINTED IN THE NETHERLANDS

To the Jacksons:
Bernard, Rosalyn, Iain and Judith

TABLE OF CONTENTS

Foreword	IX
Author's Preface	XI
Lecture I: Conversion to Judaism and Early Christianity	1
Excursus	33
Lecture II: Error and Ignorance as Excuses in Crime	49
Excursus	70
Lecture III: The Form is the Message	71
Excursus 1	117
Excursus 2	123

FOREWORD

To inaugurate the Norman and Sadie Lee Program in Jewish and Western Civilization, the University of Judaism was honored to present Professor David Daube for a series of three lectures on Jewish law. Professor Daube dealt with this subject in his usual insightful and illuminating manner and the University decided to make these lectures available to the larger public. In addition to shedding light on the themes with which they deal, Dr. Daube's lectures serve as an illustration of the kind of study to which the Lee Program is dedicated, as it seeks to present Jewish culture in the context of world civilization.

David L. Lieber, President
The University of Judaism
at Los Angeles

AUTHOR'S PREFACE

About a year ago, thanks to the inspired leadership of David L. Lieber and the munificence of Norman and Sadie Lee, the University of Judaism at Los Angeles started a carefully yet imaginatively designed Program in Jewish and Western Civilization which promises to make a major contribution to religious, scholarly and educational endeavour. It is indeed the first undergraduate core curriculum which integrates the teaching of Judaica into the teaching of Western thought and institutions. I had the honour, greatly appreciated, of delivering the three opening lectures: one, on Conversion, to a general audience, one, on Error, to the academic staff engaged in the Program, and one, on Form, to members of the legal profession. Throughout my visit I was made welcome in the most generous and helpful way by President and Mrs. Lieber and their marvellous circle; and it was a constant joy to experience the brilliance, dedication and sense of community among both teachers and students of the University. Since then I have received much encouragement from the President in committing the lectures to writing. As if they had not done enough already, Mr. and Mrs. Lee are providing a substantial subsidy towards publication. I am deeply grateful to these friends.

The following earlier work of mine will not be quoted except for special reasons.

I. Conversion to Judaism and early Christianity. – 1. The New Testament and Rabbinic Judaism, 1956, repr. 1973, pp. 106 ff. – 2. Pauline Contributions to a Pluralistic Culture: Re-creation and Beyond, in Jesus and Man's Hope, ed. D. G. Miller and D. Y. Hadidian, 1971, vol. 2, pp. 223 ff. – 3. Biblical Landmarks in the Struggle for Women's Rights, Juridical Review, vol. 90 (n.s. 23), 1978, pp. 184 ff.

Excursus. 1. The New Testament etc., pp. 27 ff. – 2. Lawless Women in the Bible, Lecture at Jerusalem Congress of Jewish Studies 1961 (unpublished). – 3. La Femme dans le Droit Biblique, Lecture at Institut de Droit Romain, Paris, 1962 (unpubl.). – 4. Edinburgh Gifford Lectures 1962 on The Deed and the Doer in the Bible (unpubl.), no. 9, Women. – 5. The Last Chapter of Esther, Jewish Quarterly Review, vol. 37, 1946, pp. 139 ff. – 6. Purim, Lecture at Congregation Beth-Sholom, San Francisco, 1972 (unpubl.).

II. Error and Ignorance as Excuses in Crime. – 1. Das Blutrecht des Alten Testaments, Göttingen Dr.Jur. dissertation, 1932 (unpubl.). – 2. Error and Accident in the Bible, Revue Internationale des Droits de l'Antiquité, vol. 2, 1949, pp. 189 ff. – 3. Sin, Ignorance and Forgiveness, Claude Montefiore Lecture 1960. – 4.

'For they know not what they do': Luke 23.34, Studia Patristica, vol. 79, 1961, pp. 58 ff. – 5. Gifford Lectures 1962 etc., no. 3, Error and Ignorance. – 6. Gifford Lectures 1963 on Law and Wisdom in the Scriptures (unpubl.), no. 4, Justice in the Narratives.

III. The Form is the Message. – I have discussed 'If' and 'He who' in Das Blutrecht etc. and in Forms of Roman Legislation, 1956, repr. 1979, pp. 6 ff.; 'Thou shalt' in a Lecture at the Oxford Society of Historical Theology, Abstract of Proceedings 1945, pp. 38 f.; Rules stated as Facts in the same Lecture, pp. 43 ff., in Appended Note to E. G. Selwyn, The First Epistle of St. Peter, 1946, 2nd ed. 1947, pp. 467 ff., and in Forms of Roman Legislation, pp. 68 ff.; 'You have heard' in The New Testament etc., pp. 55 ff.; the Fifth Commandment in Lectures (unpubl.) at Institute of Jewish Studies, Manchester, 1955, and at Department of Hebrew, University College, London, 1957, and in Gifford Lectures 1963 etc., no. 1, The Fifth Commandment, and no. 2, Deuteronomy; Diagnosis in Lecture at the Oxford Society etc., pp. 39 ff.; Technique and Technician in Lecture at NEH Seminar of Karen Lebaqcz, Berkeley, on Bioethics and Professional Responsibility, 1980 (unpubl.); and Curses in Das Blutrecht etc. and in Lecture at the Oxford Society etc., p. 39.

LECTURE I

CONVERSION TO JUDAISM AND EARLY CHRISTIANITY

1.

To begin with, two general remarks.

First, Jewish religion and Jewish peoplehood are co-extensive, having their common root in Abraham's response to the divine call.[1] Conversion, therefore, means naturalization and vice versa. This has not changed from the era of the patriarchs to this day; and attempts since the nineteenth century to split up the two have remained confined to the fringe. To be sure, one aspect or the other may be more conspicuous in different epochs or settings.

As King Ahab's wife, Queen Jezebel is an Israelitess—despite her never-wavering adherence to her Zidonian idolatry. Actually, the latter now renders her doubly guilty.[2] Conversely, though someone adopts the Jewish faith and customs, or their essentials at any rate, he or she is not Jewish so long as they continue aside from the nation. Jethro, Moses's father-in-law, while acknowledging God, remains a Midianite in Midian.[3] The Midianite Hobab becomes a resident alien in Moses's camp, but still not a Hebrew.[4] Rahab of Jericho, who harbours Joshua's spies, acknowledges God and, when Jericho is sacked, is spared with her kinsfolk to stay on as resident aliens.[5] The Syrian commander Naaman, cured of leprosy by Elisha, acknowledges God and, indeed, decides even when back in his country to sacrifice to him only; yet even he is merely a god-fearing gentile.[6] So are the Kings Nebuchadnezzar and Darius who, moved by the insight of Jewish counsellors and the miraculous survival of Jews in a furnace and a lion's den, acknowledge God, going as far as to order their subjects to worship him.[7]

---

[1] Genesis 12 ff.
[2] I Kings 16 ff.
[3] Exodus 18.11, 27.
[4] Numbers 10.29 ff.
[5] Joshua 2.11, 6.25.
[6] II Kings 5.15, 17 ff.
[7] Daniel 2.46 f., 3.28 f., 6.26 ff.

In Rabbinic literature, most of these worthies are represented as proselytes proper.[8] But, then, the assumption is that they do more than is recorded in the Bible and fulfil all conditions for becoming Jewish—both religiously and nationally. In the case of Rahab, this interpretation as well as legends depicting heaven's reward for her assistance to the Hebrews[9] are demonstrably B.C.: she ranks as an ancestress of Jesus in Matthew.[10] The Rabbinic exegesis, while anachronistic, supports rather than contradicts my thesis: conversion inevitably brings you into the religion and people at the same time.

My second reflection is this. From the earliest times, the procedure of becoming a Jew is dominated by a distinction between the sexes: the chief requirement for males is circumcision, inapplicable to females. Hence the step is incomparably easier for the latter than the former. (This is no longer so true of the better classes in Britain and British America, where circumcision of babies has become widespread. But my general argument is not thereby affected. The practice, by the way, doubtless originated, partly at least, under Scriptural influence.) It is not accidental that Jesus's genealogy in Matthew[11] includes two female converts—Rahab and Ruth—but, unless we count Abraham, no male one. That, historically, as just observed, Rahab does not qualify is immaterial: the evangelist, resting on Rabbinic tradition, sees her in the same light as Ruth. There is no male counterpart.

If it were the other way round, if things were vastly more convenient for males than females, surely the spokespersons of women's liberation would treat it as flagrant discrimination. To this, they might perhaps reply that the motive behind the advantageous position of females is not respect for them but, on the contrary, contempt. However, for one thing, this is definitely not the whole explanation: a, so far at least, intractable physical difference, for instance, also plays a part. For another, in areas where women are put down, very wisely the protesters will no longer accept alibis in the form of 'it is meant for their good'. Sauce for the gander, please: the fact is that, for whatever reasons, in the matter of becoming Jewish, females are spared a formidable obstacle.

---

[8] E.g. Mekhilta on Exodus 18.1.
[9] E.g. Siphra on Numbers 10.29, Babylonian Megillah 14b.
[10] Matthew 1.5.
[11] Matthew 1.1ff.

Its role is illumined in a dramatic fashion by the division between Judaism and Christianity. Had the apostles not abolished the requirement of circumcision, there would today be no Christianity separate from Judaism. This measure of theirs facilitated the coming over *en masse* of males as well as females; with the result that the open branch, those for whom Jesus was the Messiah, grew into a world religion, while the other one, those who did not share this belief, remained a self-contained, small group. It is, incidentally, the compactness of Judaism which has helped to preserve the primitive identity of conversion and naturalization which I have been stressing.

2.

Now for a survey of the evolution of the procedure, or rather, the main currents. There is throughout, I would caution, far more fluidity than may appear from my summary.

The fundamental division is between the period before the Babylonian exile and that from the exile onwards. In the pre-exilic era, a man becomes Jewish by circumcision. A woman's description follows her father's or husband's. As a rule, therefore, she becomes Jewish by marriage—as, in many modern states still, a foreign woman marrying a citizen by that fact obtains citizenship. It may, however, also happen when she lives in the paternal home or when she is the wife of a gentile, by her father or husband becoming Jewish. This will be an extremely rare occurrence. Yet what is, in a sense, the prototype of conversion shows the principle at work: the circumcision of Abraham and the males among his household brings into the fold the females, without further ado.[12]

Another episode in the Book of Genesis belongs here.[13] Jacob's sons propose to the Hivites of Shechem a tribal merger, really a joining of Jacob's family by the Hivites. True, they do so in bad faith, indeed, with murderous intent, but this is not here relevant. If all Hivite males, they declare, undergo circumcision, 'we will give our daughters to you and take your daughters to us, and we will dwell with you and we will become one people'.[14] Evidently,

---

[12] Genesis 17.9 ff.
[13] Genesis 34.1 ff.
[14] Genesis 34.16.

no ceremony is necessary for the Shechemite females. They automatically participate in their men's change of status.

A man, then, while having to take a hurdle a woman need not fear, once he does achieve naturalization pulls his female establishment along with him; and if the men of a tribe convert *en bloc*, the tribe, men and women, becomes Hebrew. A woman's naturalization affects no one else: at this stage, it is just an aspect of her subordination. The point always to remember is that the hurdle is enormous. There is this proviso, too, that, even in a patriarchy, a woman may have some say as to whom she is going to marry—a number of stories illustrate different degrees of such power[15]—so a switch of peoplehood would not be against her will.

Naturalization by marriage is contemplated by a Deuteronomic statute[16] concerning a prisoner of war. 'You shall bring her into your house, and she shall shave her head and pare her nails and put her raiment of captivity from off her and stay in your house and bewail her father and mother a full month; and after that you shall possess her and she shall be to wife to you'. The rites all symbolize separation, be it from her origin, be it from her prisoner's condition. None symbolizes incorporation: marriage does that. In this case, plainly, she is not asked.

Marrying a heathen is frequently branded as evil—Deuteronomy itself warns against it[17]—and heathen women figure much more prominently in these and allied texts than heathen men.[18] Nevertheless the marriage with a heathen woman is valid, the offspring fully legitimate. The two tribes of Ephraim and Manasseh descend from Joseph's union with the daughter of an Egyptian priest.[19] Moses's father-in-law is a Midianite priest.[20] Rehoboam is a son of Solomon and an Ammonitess, Ahaziah and Jehoram are sons of Ahab and the Zidonian Jezebel. All three succeed to the throne without any difficulty on account of the mother's provenance.[21] It is significant that, while quite a few Biblical names refer to the father,

---

[15] Genesis 24.15 ff., I Samuel 25.
[16] Deuteronomy 21.10 ff.
[17] Deuteronomy 7.3; cp. Judges 3.6.
[18] Genesis 24.3, 26.35, 27.46, 28.1, Exodus 34.16, Numbers 12.1, 25.1 ff., I Kings 11.2, 16.31. On Ezra and Nehemiah, see below. pp. 7 ff.
[19] Genesis 41.50 ff.
[20] Exodus 2.21; cp. Numbers 12.1.
[21] I Kings 14.21, II Chronicles 12.13, I Kings 16.31, 22.40, 52 f., II Kings 3.1 f.

Abigail for example, none refers to the mother. This matter, however, I shall not pursue.

A reservation is called for: we must not make the rules too rigid. Apart from the existence of various types of marriage, with various legal effects—if a foreign woman marries a Jew or, for that matter, if a Jewess marries out, her husband dies or divorces her and there is no offspring, she may re-acquire her original nationality. We shall presently find this exemplified in the Book of Ruth. A parallel is provided by a priest's daughter who, on marrying a layman, ceases to be entitled to sanctified food, but regains her fitness if she returns under her father's roof, childless, after termination of the marriage.[22] (The situation of Judah's daughter-in-law Tamar at a certain stage[23] shows how complicated things can be; I shall not here go into it.) The conduct of the son of an Egyptian living among the Israelites and an Israelitess gives rise, we learn in the Pentateuch,[24] to legislation about blasphemy. He shares his father's status, and the law promulgated expressly threatens 'as well the stranger as the home-born'.[25] The same status would attach to his mother. By contrast, Bath-sheba, who bears no child to her Hittite husband Uriah, on his death can marry David as a Jewess. The marriage would have re-naturalized her in any case.[26]

In the Book of Ruth,[27] Elimelech, a Judean, because of a famine, goes to live for a while in Moab, with his wife Naomi and their two sons Sickly and Weakly. He dies. His sons marry natives, Orpah and Ruth, who automatically enter the family.

However, the young men, too, now die, without children. For the moment, Naomi is more or less head of the house and, the famine having ended, she resolves to move back to Judah. Orpah—I quote—'returns to her people and to her gods', thereby reassuming her native Moabite status. Ruth follows Naomi: 'Your people is my people and your God is my God'.[28] No doubt she remains part of the group. Incidentally, the unity of nation and religion could not be expressed more clearly.

---

[22] Leviticus 22.12f.
[23] Genesis 38.11.
[24] Leviticus 24.10ff.
[25] Leviticus 24.16.
[26] II Samuel 11.
[27] See Excursus, below, pp. 33ff.
[28] Ruth 1.15f.

To be sure, in the narrative, the epithet 'the Moabitess' sticks to her.[29] At one time, I thought it might not mean much more than when my colleagues call me a German. But it does: there is the implication of a very special loyalty on the part of that lady from abroad. To recapitulate: in this epoch, a woman's religion is determined by her father's or husband's—except where she got into the group by marriage and the marriage ends without children. In these, obviously most uncommon, circumstances, she decides. A mere woman, she may opt for her present affiliation or her former one. That is dramatic enough, but Ruth's choice is all the more so since, up to now, she never set foot outside the country of her birth. Rebekkah journeys into a distant land in order to marry Isaac,[30] and Israel follows the Lord, her bridegroom, into the wilderness.[31] Here a stranger married to an Israelite even after his death accompanies his mother into the, to her, quite unknown Judah. The Moabitess who has freely, trustingly, preferred her new allegiance—that is what the attribute conveys. It is anything but an empty phrase.

On the other hand, it in no way suggests that she is not Jewish. At her first meeting in Judah with Sickly's and Weakly's sturdier relation Boaz, Pillar, he congratulates her on 'leaving your father and mother and the land of your nativity and coming unto a people which you did not know heretofore', and blesses her, 'a full reward be given you of the Lord God of Israel under whose wings you are come to trust'—again, note, people and God figuring equally. In fact, he ends by marrying her as belonging to Elimelech's estate which he redeems, i.e. saves from falling into the hands of outsiders.[32]

Throughout the story, no rite of reception is alluded to. A woman is received through marriage. If widowed and childless, retention or loss of her acquired nationality depends on whether she stays or returns to her kin. Certainly, the Rabbis, as mentioned already, take compliance with their requirements for granted, but this is to transfer them back into a different system.

It is in fact highly remarkable that they admit to finding no Scriptural indication of baptism of female converts. Otherwise so adept

---

[29] Ruth 1.22, 2.2, 6, 21, 4.5, 10.
[30] Genesis 24.58.
[31] Jeremiah 2.2.
[32] Ruth 3.10 ff., 4.1 ff.

in interpreting the old writings their way, here they concede. They do, of course, none the less manage to prove its early existence: it is demonstrable, we are assured, by logic, nearly as good as a text. The precise reasoning offered is the rather desperate one from *reductio ad absurdum*: in the absence of such a ceremony, there would have been, they claim, no means of gathering in the female part of the people when the Sinaitic community was founded—a conclusion impossible to contemplate.[33]

During a brief visit with the Samaritans at Nablus, I enquired about their regulations and was informed that marriage is, and has always been, enough to incorporate a woman. I was delighted for, if correct, it is of manifest relevance.

3.

In the exile, the archaic regime proves inadequate; and above all, the part of it relating to females. Jewry is a tiny band on alien soil, in the midst of a grand pagan civilisation, to assimilate to which is a constant temptation. In these conditions, when a Jew marries a gentile woman, quite likely, far from her joining his set, he will do his best to go over to hers and be lost to his own. You will not need my help to think of modern parallels. Marriage itself, therefore, can no longer be deemed to incorporate a woman in the fold. To achieve this effect, a special act is required that brings her over as a person, on the basis of a decision: baptism. How far the choice of this rite is due to the Biblical instances of immersion, how far to Babylonian cults, I shall not here inquire.

My explanation of the development is strongly supported by the fact that, as soon as resettlement in the holy land gets under way, the laxer method comes to the fore again and women from the local tribes are introduced into the community by marriage. There is no longer the all-pervasive fear of being swallowed up by the surrounding culture. Ezra and Nehemiah, however, both having grown up and reached eminence in Persia, on taking charge of affairs in the land voice the most intransigent opposition.[34] The men are given the choice between dismissing their wives, together with any children, and being excluded themselves from the new-founded

---

[33] Babylonian Yebamoth 46a. On the nature of *reductio*, see my *Roman Law*, 1969, pp. 176 ff.
[34] Ezra 9 f., Nehemiah 13.23 ff.

state. This dismissal is not by a regular bill of divorce,[35] which presupposes a valid marriage and mentions the woman's freedom to conclude a fresh one. Ezra and Nehemiah recognize no tie with these women and none, in consequence, with the children. Something of an analogy is furnished by the contrast between the unwillingness of the pre-world-war II German and British Rabbinates to receive converts and the relaxed attitude in Israel.[36] I daresay the diehards I knew at Frankfurt am Main and London, if they could take over at Jerusalem and Tel-Aviv today, might carry out a few evictions.

Anyhow, a corollary of the new dispensation is that a woman can convert on her own, without marriage. Before then, it is marriage or her father's or husband's conversion that naturalizes her. Henceforth, at least one who is not under a man's *potestas*—say, a widow whose father is dead—may make up her mind to embrace Judaism and be baptized. That this must profoundly change the entire atmosphere of conversion stands to reason. Conviction will often be the dominant factor, the emphasis shifting from change of peoplehood to change of religion—only the emphasis: both are still firmly linked. Furthermore, it is a landmark in the advance of women towards influence and power. Under the old system, we have seen, about the only situation where a woman can independently document her faith is that of Ruth; and her saga shows with what gratitude adherence—not, in strictness, conversion, but adherence—to the Hebrew side is appreciated. From now, there is far more opportunity for women to take a stand.

Before long, the requirement of baptism is extended to males, added to circumcision. Presumably the idea of regeneration attaching to baptism acquires such weight that confinement to one sex is intolerable. At any rate, the factors that bring about a reception rite for women affect also the conversion of males: increasingly, attention focuses on its religious element, and in particular, on submission to the commandments. In the midst of a foreign environment, their observance becomes absolutely essential to the preservation of the group. That their centrality is upheld after the return is due to

---

[35] See my *Pauline Contributions*, p. 244 n. 79, and *Civil Disobedience in Antiquity*, 1972, p. 16 n. 4.
[36] Since writing this, I have found confirmation in a review by E. L. Ehrlich of J. R. Rosenbloom, *Conversion to Judaism*, 1978, in *Freiburger Rundbrief*, vol. 31, 1979, p. 141.

the efforts of Ezra and Nehemiah.[37] Even so, re-settlement in time permits a good deal of laxity until the loss of statehood in A.D. 70 produces a renewed concentration on strict practice. Once more, the contemporary scene is illuminating: it is easier to go for an outing in your car on the Day of Atonement and remain a Jew in Israel than in Britain.

It is during the exile, then, that naturalization comes to mean entry not only into the Abrahamic covenant but also into the Sinaitic one. Abraham goes on being 'the father of proselytes'.[38] Even in our day, a male convert's Hebrew name describes him, not as 'son of John or Henry', his physical father, but as 'son of Abraham', and traditionally a female convert is called 'daughter of Abraham'.[39] (Though 'daughter of Sarah' seems to be making headway.[40]) At the same time, the requirements of conversion are based by the Rabbis on what, in their belief (or that of a majority), had been demanded of the people assembled at Sinai: as for the males, circumcision, baptism and a sacrifice, as for the females, the latter two. For the purpose in hand, it does not matter that this doctrine involves much tortuous reasoning as well as forced interpretation of the Biblical record. The sacrifice, of course, drops out with the destruction of the second Temple.[41]

In the preparation of a would-be convert, the Torah coming from Sinai now plays a conspicuous part. The initial link of this component with the introduction of baptism—both called forth by the exigencies of exile and reconstruction under Ezra and Nehemiah—leaves permanent traces. A representative sample of the commandments, for instance, is to be recited, the Rabbis lay down,[42] during the actual immersion. This may be the place to add that the Talmudic regulation[43] that baptism must take place before witnesses or even a court looks like another consequence of the situation in exile, when the community needs to be assured in this way where the person stands. Previously, there is in general no problem about clarity.

---

[37] Nehemiah 8.
[38] Midrash Tanhuma on Genesis 14.1. Cp. Matthew 3.9 to be quoted presently.
[39] Cp. Babylonian Ketuboth 72b, Gittin 89a, Luke 13.16.
[40] See C. G. Montefiore and H. Loewe, *A Rabbinic Anthology*, 1938, repr. 1974, p. 574.
[41] Babylonian Keritoth 9a, Yebamoth 46a f.
[42] Babylonian Yebamoth 47b.
[43] Babylonian Yebamoth 46b f.

By New Testament times, proselyte baptism for both sexes has gone on for centuries. It is so established an institution that John the Baptist can transfer it to the inner mission, the call to Jews to become true, end-time Jews, aimed at men at least as much as women. This proselytizing of those already within is the novel feature of his activity (which does not exclude earlier adumbrations, say, among the Dead Sea monks) accounting for the epithet 'Baptizer' or 'Baptist' bestowed on him. An agent noun tends to be employed where the action indicated by the verb is performed in an extraordinary fashion.[44] We all dream, but it is when you are absent-minded during an important meeting or absorbed in thought in the middle of a busy road that your are called 'a dreamer'. Nothing remarkable in baptizing a gentile entering Judaism. But John proclaims that even the Jews must enter: 'Think not, We have Abraham to father',[45] i.e., you must acquire him just like strangers. It is when he baptizes even Jews that he becomes 'the Baptizer', 'the Baptist'.

That nature of his baptism as proselyte baptism comes out in details.[46] The precise moment at which a gentile becomes Jewish is when emerging from the water: 'He immerses and comes up—behold, he is like an Israelite in all respects'.[47] Accordingly, Mark,[48] in reporting Jesus's baptism by John, tells us: 'And at once, coming out of the water, he saw the heavens rent and the Spirit descending'. In passing, Josephus relates[49] that John exhorted the Jews to practise righteousness and undergo baptism, and that Herod became alarmed 'when others gathered with them'. Who these others may have been is a longstanding puzzle. Could it be gentiles? Luke[50] seems to assume that some joined the crowd—though, considering his pronounced inclination to universalism, this is not the strongest evidence.

---

[44] See my *Roman Law*, 1969, pp. 2ff.
[45] Matthew 3.9.
[46] See my *New Testament and Rabbinic Judaism*, pp. 111f., and *The Sudden in the Scriptures*, 1964, pp. 46f.
[47] Babylonian Yebamoth 47b.
[48] Mark 1.10.
[49] Josephus, *Jewish Antiquities* 18.5.2.117f.
[50] Luke 3.14. 'Nothing to show whether the soldiers are Jewish soldiers of Antipas or Romans under the Procurator': J. M. Creed, *The Gospel according to St. Luke*, 1930, p. 53. But even Antipas's soldiers would most probably include non-Jews: K. H. Rengstorf, *Das Evangelium nach Lukas*, 9th ed., 1962, p. 57, with reference to Josephus, *Jewish Antiquities* 17.8.3.198.

4.

By the opening of the current era, Judaism exercises a strong attraction. The possession of the Old Testament may well be a major factor. It is consistent with this explanation that Jewish-Christian preaching has had scant success in the East—India, China—with comprehensive religious Scriptures of its own. (In my opinion, the predominance of Roman law from the Middle Ages on owes more to its availability in a written corpus than to quality. *Denn was man schwarz auf weiss besitzt,* Goethe has a trusting young student believe,[51] *Kann man getrost nach Hause tragen.*) Anyhow there are many women converts[52] and many god-fearing men, men who, short of circumcision, conduct themselves as Jews.[53] For Schürer, the numerical superiority of full proselytesses over full proselytes bespeaks the female heart's susceptibility to religious movements.[54] Something in this, no doubt. But I wonder whether the statistics would not look a bit different if a woman wishing to be received had, say, to turn into an Amazon.[55] An article by Pope presents a sound picture.[56]

In a culture where surgical instruments are crude by our standards and there is neither anaesthetis nor antisepsis, circumcision is a gruesome prospect for an adult. The Pentateuch itself, in the narrative about Shechem,[57] regards ill-effects as common. 'And it came to pass on the third day, when they were suffering, that' and so on;[58] the suffering is referred to in a subordinate clause, it is not an extraordinary result that would deserve a main one. In Matthew,[59] the scribes and Pharisees are said to 'compass sea and land to make one proselyte'. This testifies to intense missionary

---

[51] Goethe, *Faust*, Part 1, Schülerszene.
[52] E.g. Josephus, *Jewish War* 2.20.2.560.
[53] E.g. Josephus, *Jewish Antiquities* 14.7.2.110.
[54] See E. Schürer, *Geschichte des Jüdischen Volkes im Zeitalter Jesu Christi*, 2nd ed., pt. 2, 1886, p. 561: *Am meisten erwiesen sich auch hier, wie bei jeder religiösen Bewegung, die Frauenherzen empfänglich.*
[55] Cp. Kleist, *Penthesilea*, Scene 15: *Doch als die feige Regung um sich griff, Riss sie die rechte Brust sich ab und taufte Die Frauen, die den Bogen spannen würden, Und sank zusammen, eh' sie noch vollendet: Die Amazonen oder Busenlosen!* — *Hierauf ward ihr die Krone aufgesetzt.*
[56] See M. H. Pope, in *The Interpreter's Dictionary of the Bible*, vol. 3, 1962, p. 928.
[57] See above, pp. 3 f.
[58] Genesis 34.25.
[59] Matthew 23.15.

longings but not, as often thought,[60] to signal success. On the contrary, one senses a note of despair in respect of the chances of winning male converts. The very occasional break—and we do hear of several[61]—is such a triumph that no effort is too great. (I am discounting enforced conversions which did happen, though rarely.[62] Josephus disapproves.[63]) Billy Graham need not fly from one continent to the other to gain one soul. A friend of mine does it: he is looking for supporters of an Institute of Ancient Jewish Law to be founded—and funded.

From Josephus we learn[64] that a prince of Commagene, betrothed to Drusilla, daughter of Agrippa I, in the end withdrew, unwilling to convert; whereupon she was given to the king of Emeza 'who had consented to be circumcised'. Apparently, circumcision more than anything else was the stumbling-block. Drusilla finished up as the procurator Felix's wife.[65]

When the apostles decree[66] that baptism suffices for men no less than women, mass proselytization becomes feasible. A man need no longer be in dread of that operation. Even women will find the step more comfortable: previously, quite a few inclined to take it would hold back since their husbands could not—or not easily—join them.

To some extent at least, it must be under the impact of Christianity's enviable progress that the Hillelite sage Joshua ben Hananiah, around A.D. 100, takes up the same position: a male gentile, like a female one, is Jewish as soon as baptized. Yet not quite the same: whereas in Christianity circumcision is definitely abandoned, for Joshua it does remain an inescapable duty. A proselyte not circumcised in the course of coming over is obliged to get circumcised after. If he is remiss, then, though he is a Jew—or precisely because he is one—he is comitting a terrible sin.

---

[60] See E. Schürer, *op. cit.*, p. 558.

[61] King Izates of Adiabene, Josephus, *Jewish Antiquities* 20.2.4.46; Onkelos, *Babylonian Gittin* 56b f., etc.

[62] E.g. Josephus, *Jewish Antiquities* 13.11.3.318.

[63] Josephus, *Life* 23.113. That routine circumcision—or baptism—of children or youngsters within the group is enforced was not then realized; it is barely beginning to be realized today. To be clear about it does not, of course, necessarily mean rejection. For some comments of mine on unwanted salvation, see *Humanities in Society*, vol. 2, 1979, pp. 74 ff.

[64] Josephus, *Jewish Antiquities* 20.7.1.139.

[65] Acts 24.24.

[66] Acts 15.

Joshua's suggestion is allowed a fair trial run. This is reflected in a paragraph in the Talmud representing—implausibly—his more rigid colleague Eliezer ben Hyrcanus as agreeing; a preceding summary shows him in his usual role. The concession, however, is much too limited to restore the balance. By the end of the second century, the majority has decisively turned against it, insisting on circumcision as indispensable to conversion.[67] If 'the fountain' in Juvental's antisemitic lines alludes to baptism, he is depicting the early, uncompromising stand: Moses, he says, commanded 'to conduct to the fountain solely the circumcised'.[68]

More and more, the purest dedication to God and his Torah is expected of a candidate. A woman's intent to wed a Jew is listed by the Rabbis among the inadequate stimuli: ironical, considering that, prior to the exile, marriage is the regular route by which she enters the nation. R. Nehemiah, a survivor of the Hadrianic persecution, voices the extreme view that not only should a person prompted by love not be accepted, but if, despite this bar, the procedure is gone through—circumcision and baptism in the case of a man, baptism in that of a woman—it is invalid.[69]

The motive of ʾahabha, by the way, passes through revealing stages. Basically, the word signifies 'love'; but as in the present context it refers to non-sexual emotions—non-sexual as viewed by the Rabbis, unacquainted with Freud—we had better speak of 'friendship' or 'affection'. (The Mishnah contrasts the object-oriented ʾahabha between Amnon and Tamar with the pure one between David and Jonathan.[70]) In the Palestinian Talmud, friendship with a Jew or Jewess figures side by side with intent to marry, an improper ground for conversion.[71] The Babylonian Talmud omits it.[72] Not, surely, because of a more favourable assessment, but because it no longer belongs to the world of experience. In the post-Talmudic tractate on Proselytes[73] it is paired off as unsatisfactory, not with intent to marry, but with fear of the Jews, of which

---

[67] Babylonian Yebamoth 56a f. Cp. L. H. Feldman, in *The Loeb Classical Library's Josephus*, vol. 9, 1965, pp. 410 f.
[68] Juvenal, *Satires* 14.104.
[69] Babylonian Yebamoth 24b.
[70] Mishnah Aboth 5.16, II Samuel 13, I Samuel 18 ff.
[71] Palestinian Qiddushin 65b.
[72] Babylonian Yebamoth 24b.
[73] Gerim 1.7.

the Book of Esther supplies the chief precedent.[74] A. Cohen rightly concludes that what is envisaged is not personal friendship, but appreciation of the Jews at large. The tractate puts it as a foil to fear—both, of course, by this time quite academic. Apparently, however, Cohen cannot bear even the theoretical rejection of a gentile with a genuine enthusiasm for Jewry. So he adds that he is 'perhaps deriving material advantage from his conversion'.[75]

5.

As hinted above,[76] with baptism comes in the notion of conversion as rebirth.[77] Rebirth is chic nowadays—and skindeep. When brought about by Jewish baptism, it is serious, creating a fresh child. Its effects on family are specially notable. For example, the bond between a couple who convert is dissolved: they are now different persons. To be sure, it is readily restorable by cohabitation—at least before the Rabbis, from the third century on, become more and more hostile to marriage by intercourse.[78] Again, a mother and a son who convert may marry: they are no longer related. With regard to this type of case, already in the pre-Christian epoch the sages introduce a proviso: no union must be contracted which is repudiated by the surrounding heathen society. It is in this modified form that the early Church takes over the practice. Paul[79] condemns the marriage between a stepson and stepmother among his Corinthian flock because this, he explains, 'does not pass even among the gentiles'.

The reason for the restriction transmitted in the sources is that a convert allowed to marry someone that would not be allowed under heathen law might believe Judaism to be lax in such matters and generally slip back into licentious habits. Doubtless the Rabbis also fear the impression on outsiders. As is well known, total neglect of the usual barriers is a widespread charge in antiquity against Jews and Christians. 'They abstain', Tacitus reports of the former, 'from taking foreign women; but among themselves nothing is

---

[74] Esther 8.17.
[75] See A. Cohen, *Soncino edition of Minor Tractates of the Talmud*, vol. 2, 1965, p. 604.
[76] See above, p. 8.
[77] Babylonian Yebamoth 48b.
[78] Mishnah Qiddushin 1.1, Babylonian Qiddushin 12b.
[79] I Corinthians 5.1.

illicit'.[80] A number of the latter are convicted of 'Oedipodean intercourse' at Lyons and Vienne in the second century.[81] It is universally assumed, without discussion, that it is all sheer calumny. Conrat's treatment is typical: 'It need hardly be mentioned that these accusations were groundless'.[82] But they are not—not entirely. From whom would gentiles—including relatively objective students among them—get firsthand information about the two faiths? Mainly from converts, a cousin, an aunt, who had become Jewish or Christian. And these would tell them of their freedom. Paul's Corinthian community are 'puffed up' by, proud of, their standing above the ordinary curbs between close relations—relations no longer as a result of baptism.[83] To an outsider, unappreciative of the miracle, incest is incest. Plainly, the indictment does not spring up *ex nihilo*, and counter-measures such as the one discouraging the most offensive ties are to be expected.

Conceivably, the influx of slaves also plays a part. A Roman master might breed slaves as we do terriers: the incest taboos do not apply, often a slave would have no idea of the identity of father, mother, son, daughter and so on, alliances between otherwise forbidden degrees are unavoidable and instinctive aversion to them cannot but be greatly reduced. However, this is at most a minor factor in the growth of the misunderstanding. The hostile writers definitely connect the Jews' and Christians' immorality with their religion. So it is the convert's treatment as a new being which must be chiefly responsible.

Generally speaking, propaganda against a collective cannot be successfully based on a one-hundred-percent lie; you want a grain of truth, however microscopic. If Hitler had contended that every Jew has an eye at the back of his head enabling him to watch what goes on behind him, it would not have worked. His assertion that there is no financial scandal not caused by a Jew did impress. Some smoke is needed to shout 'Fire!' with effect; and I think that the familar, gross pagan anti-Jewish and anti-Christian aspersions are none of them devoid of a minimum factual input. To work this out would be interesting from more than one point of view, but this is not the place for it.

---

[80] Tacitus, *Histories* 5.5.
[81] Eusebius, *Ecclesiastical History* 5.1.14.
[82] See M. Conrat, *Die Christenverfolgungen im Römischen Reiche*, 1897, p. 31.
[83] I Corinthians 5.2.

There is absolute agreement in literature that Jewish proselyte baptism does not possess sacramental character. I do not like disputing about nomenclature. But I would be curious to hear a definition of 'sacramental' excluding an act so powerful as this one. Christianity, as it spreads outward, forgets about and sheds the full implications of re-creation. Judaism still acknowledges them. When I was young, Jewish scholarship rather avoided dealing with them. They could by no manner of rationalization be reconciled with, made palatable to, the then prevalent climate of Western theology. Things move fast. Some ten years ago, preparing a book that never appeared, I wrote: 'If there were an isolated part of the globe where, for instance, marriage between brother and sister were tolerated, and a gentile family adopted the Jewish faith, such a marriage would be in order even today'. We need no longer be so hypothetical. Sweden may soon provide the Rabbinate with a case testing the doctrine. It is, of course, not a reawakened Norse belief in true renewal but a devaluation of kinship that makes it easier for us to come out of the closet.

Paul, I have just pointed out, still goes along with the Jewish scheme. A remarkable illustration is furnished by the problem of a convert whose spouse does not join in.[84] The marriage, he teaches, is terminated: the convert is a new person. None the less, if the unbeliever is content to stay on, that ought to be accepted. Cohabitation will 'consecrate' him or her, will bring about a fresh marriage—preferable to a casting off. Not surprisingly, from the early Middle Ages on, the argument, proceeding as it does from the Rabbinic estimate of rebirth, has been totally misunderstood, the outcome being the so-called Pauline privilege.

In support of his advice not to oust the unbeliever, Paul names two motives: peace and the hope that, ultimately, he or she may be won over. This involves a fundamental question. A convert is 'in the position of a child just born', the Rabbis hold,[85] the result of 'a new creation', in Paul's language.[86] 'The old things have gone', the latter exclaims, 'new things have come into being'. The trouble is that, in living reality, the miracle is less thorough. The whole issue

---

[84] I Corinthians 7.12 ff.
[85] Babylonian Yebamoth 48b; cp. John 3.3.
[86] II Corinthians 5.17, Galatians 6.15.

of legislation enacting an impossibility arises in this connection[87] though I shall confine myself to a few conundrums from conversion.

In the sphere of law, secular or religious, it is relatively easiest to make a fresh start. Marriage dissolved. Blood ties severed, hence no forbidden degrees, as also no claims to inheritance. And so on. But even here, difficulties crop up. Are debts cancelled? Is a slave convert free? (Needless to say, whatever the Jewish or early Christian answers, gentiles would not allow them to work to their disadvantage—which is a further complication.) Is a prostitute convert a virgin? Do children born before conversion count towards fulfillment of the duty of propagation?[88] If a proselyte who had a son before has sons again, is the new firstborn entitled to a double share of the estate?[89] May a convert recite the Avowal speaking of the land 'which the Lord swore to our Fathers for to give us'?[90] The opposite of the legal domain is the physical, where the old things will persist most stubbornly. A one-armed person remains one-armed. Milieu, in a way, belongs to the grace-resistant, physical world. A water-carrier continues a water-carrier. A Jew is suspected of an affair with a gentile woman and she converts: is marriage permissible even though it must lend colour to the rumour?[91]

In between is the area of morality in the widest sense. The two considerations advanced by Paul, peace and hope of winning another convert, pertain to milieu—public policy, to be precise. Plainly, however, he feels that, apart from them, the converting spouse does not get rid of all responsibility for the non-converting one: witness the warm directness of his appeal, 'For how do you know, O wife, if you may not save your husband, or how do you know, O husband, if you may not save your wife?'. The Rabbis[92] are exercised by the sufferings of proselytes: for what sins could they be inflicted? One solution refers to violation of the Noachian duties—natural morality—in pre-conversion life. This implies full continuation of the moral personality. Many, however, will not ad-

---

[87] See my *Pope John XXIII Lecture* in *Catholic University of American Law Review*, vol. 16, 1967, pp. 386 ff., and my *Natural Law Lecture* in *Natural Law Forum*, vol. 12, 1967, pp. 1 ff.
[88] Babylonian Yebamoth 62a.
[89] Ibid.
[90] Deuteronomy 26.3, Mishnah Bikkurim 1.4.
[91] Mishnah Yebamoth 2.8.
[92] Babylonian Yebamoth 48b.

mit this. So another explanation is that proselytes tend to comply with the commandments from fear of God rather than love, or they tend to be negligent in details—hence deserve punishment. An answer with a long history[93] places the cause in the transitional period between discovery of God and actual conversion: the sin consists in prolonged hesitation after seeing the light. Somehow, for the purpose of basic moral accountability, rebirth is pre-dated to that moment.

6.

The main phases of the baptismal instruction recommended in the Talmud[94] date from the pre-Christian period. One piece of evidence is their recurrence in the earliest Christian catechisms. This applies to both form and substance, that is to say, to both the arrangement of topics and the ideas.

The arrangement comprises five parts: test, commandments, charity, penalties, reward and world to come. Test: is the candidate suitable? Commandments: an outline of what is expected of a Jew. Charity: obligations to the poor of the community. Penalties: the responsibility incurred by a sinful Jew. Reward and world to come: the bliss in store for the righteous.

The test may look simple; it is actually of extraordinary subtlety. The applicant is to be asked: 'What have you seen that you have come in order to convert? Do you not know that Israel at this time are broken down, pushed about, driven about and tossed about, and that sufferings befall them?'. If he replies 'I know and am not worthy', no further proofs are needed. Mere willingness to conform is not enough: it must spring from the right disposition. Once that is present, on the other hand, everything will be alright.

It is quite usual for an outsider wishing to be let inside to have to prove his fitness. Rituals of initiation when a tribe or a fraternity admits a stranger or a freshman, or when the adults of a tribe admit those coming of age, are relevant; but also the long questionnaires an alien seeking naturalization must fill in and his oath of allegiance. The Essenes and the Qumran band were notoriously difficult to join.[95] Two qualifications above all tend to be looked for:

---

[93] Cp. Josephus, *Jewish Antiquities* 20.2.4.45.
[94] Babylonian Yebamoth 47 a f.
[95] Josephus, *Jewish War* 2.8.7.137 ff., *Manual of Discipline* 6.13 ff.

earnestness of the desire to join and useful attributes. A community has little interest in creating unreliable or unprofitable members. Often one test will establish both requirements. If you wanted to settle for good in medieval Podersdorf, you had to carry a huge dog through the village. This, besides being an occasion for merriment, showed you at once really determined to live just there and endowed with strength and courage.[96]

In the case of a man, circumcision is an initiatory rite placing firmness of intent beyond the shadow of a doubt. The test here inspected, which takes place before circumcision, is of much later origin and, as already noted, highly sophisticated. It is applicable to men and women alike; and it is designed to make sure not only of the keeness of intent but also of the most important attributes a member of the faith can have—a true understanding of Israel's destiny.

One feature deserves special notice. Many groups, with a view to discouraging undesirables, make entrance hard. But this test goes further. The petitioner is reminded that the very result of conversion would be unpleasant: even should all the obstacles in the way of entrance be overcome—the test itself being one of them—or precisely then, he would find himself in a miserable position, far worse off than now. The interesting point about such cautioning is that, of really serious candidates, though some may be put off by it, more will be spurred on. In fact, this line pays off in other provinces of life—as any Don Juan knows: do not let yourself in with me, I am a good-for-nothing, unfaithful, doomed, bringing sorrow wherever I step; and promptly she falls for him. Or Churchill's summons to nothing but blood, sweat and tears.

A number of factors explain the seductive effect of this kind of warning. Masochism is a widespread phenomenon. So is guilt, assuaged by sharing the fate of the underdog. So is eagerness to take up a challenge: there is an enormous genetic premium on it (so long as it is not excessive). A would-be Jew, in particular, is likely to feel that a religion whose followers are so loyal to it despite all the drawbacks advertised must be wonderful. From the warner's standpoint, it may be added, there are advantages extending to after he has gained his main object. Those won over through such negative propaganda may be inspired to disprove it and demonstrate the

---

[96] See H. Fehr, *Der Humor im Recht*, 1946, pp. 12 f.

possibility of happiness in their new state. Again, should things go wrong, he can meet reproaches by 'I told you so'.

Yet, on a deeper level, what at first sight appears to be a self-deprecatory statement is exactly the opposite: a proud reference to Israel's glory. Their afflictions are a sign of God's nearness to them: 'his name rests upon him whom chastisements befall'.[97] Moreover, the saintly individual who suffers may be sure of inheriting the world to come;[98] while the nation's woes presage the final deliverance. 'Israel at this time are broken down': at this time, which will presently give way to a new aeon. The ideal catechumen is to understand all this. Given due intimation of the terrible things awaiting him, he responds: 'I know and am not worthy'.

One could look on the test as exemplifying the Rabbinic dictum that 'ever the left hand should thrust away and the right hand draw near'.[99] The right hand, of course, is the stronger one. A beautiful adumbration of the design is supplied by Naomi's speeches to her widowed daughters-in-law as they have to choose between returning to their original kinsfolk and cleaving to her. One, in the end, heeds her grim predictions and leaves—and there is not the slightest adverse comment made on it. As the other proves 'absolutely steadfast', Naomi desists from further dissuasion and takes her with her to Judah. This one becomes the ancestress of the house of David.[100]

7.

On the remaining heads of the catechism I have so little to add to what I have said elsewhere that I shall not waste your time over them. Instead, let me append a note as to my dating of the material. Far from being comprehensive, it will be confined to two points often neglected. My reason for bringing them up is that they answer, I trust, two questions raised by my friend Morton Smith in a letter concerning a previous publication of mine.[101]

---

[97] Mekhilta on Exodus 20.23.
[98] Babylonian Qiddushim 40b, Syriac Apocalypse of Baruch 52.6.
[99] Babylonian Sotah 47a.
[100] Ruth 1.8ff., 4.17.
[101] *Pauline Contributions to a Pluralistic Culture: Re-Creation and Beyond, Jesus and Man's Hope*, vol. 2, Pittsburgh, 1971 (ed. D. G. Miller and D. Y. Hadidian), pp. 223 ff.

Point one is loosely connected with the famous criterion of the *lectio difficilior*: we must pay attention to the greater or lesser attractiveness of an idea as time goes on. More precisely, if an idea is in conformity with 'progress', we want strong evidence before being sure it is old; whereas the opposite presumption applies to an idea that is awkward to accommodate. Smith asks me why I take the exemption of a convert to Judaism from the normal laws of incest to be of early origin. My reply is that—quite apart from other indications such as the Pauline epistles I have quoted and the cultural background of the Talmudic cases—this admission of what to any unlearned onlooker must seem the ghastliest perversity cannot but come down from a remote epoch. Already for the Tannaites, it becomes palpably more and more difficult to take. It would not have been set going, say, any time A.D. It goes back to B.C., and the Rabbis are busy watering it down. As a parallel—even if we looked at nothing but twentieth-century evidence, it would be safe to conclude that the ceremony of Halizah [102] was not a modern invention: the discomfort with it is so marked.

Point two: we must distinguish between the—relatively—stable essentials of a piece as our chief guidance and the variable incidentals that may come from any moment in the course of its transmission. Towards the end of the Odyssey, the hero is said to have come though he has come late. The same is said in Schiller's Die Piccolomini of Count Isolan. The gist of the remark remains due to Homer even after the substitution of a different person and different circumstances.[103] In discussing relations with outsiders, I have maintained that primitive Christianity inherits from Judaism a combination of two aims: that of harmony with them and that of eliciting their admiration or even winning them over. As a Jewish model I cite the conduct of Simeon ben Shetah, of the first half of the first century B.C., who, though not strictly obliged to do so, returns to a heathen a pearl mistakenly delivered, because 'he prefers hearing the Saracene say, Blessed be the God of the Jews, to all the gain of this world'.[104] But, Smith objects, Saracenes figure in Greek sources from the third century A.D. only: so can this anecdote be older? Yes, it can, and considering what we know about its

---

[102] Deuteronomy 25.9.
[103] Homer, *Odyssey* 23.7, Schiller, *Die Piccolomini* 1.1; see G. Büchmann, *Geflügelte Worte*, 26th ed. by B. Krieger, 1920, p. 188.
[104] Palestinian Baba Metzia 8c.

protagonist and his milieu, it may safely be treated as, on the whole, reliable—indeed, it fits no other period half as well. Only a Saracene is substituted for some other foreigner in prior versions: such a change keeps a story alive, up to date. Wherever possible, in regaling my class at Boalt Hall with legends I heard long ago about Cambridge or Oxford dons, I replace them by my present confrères; yet the Camford character of the quips is scarcely affected.

Basically, Plautus's Comedy of Asses is, as he says, a play by Demophilos, though many of the witticisms are Plautine. When I worked on fables, I was amused by the transformation of animals in the course of migration. The longbeaked bird that removes a bone from the wolf's throat is a heron, a waterfowl, in Babrius's Greek version, a crane in Phaedrus's Latin one, a stork in La Fontaine. Joshua ben Hananiah speaks of an Egyptian partridge; and the wolf becomes a lion—symbolizing Rome or the Emperor Hadrian.[105] None the less the body of the paradigm stays the same throughout. This is not to deny that, when we trace the career of a doctrine or a tale, the slightest modification may be immensely significant. For correct and full use, however, it must be set precisely against the original, main part. What is truly Plautine about the Comedy of Asses cannot possibly be seen if the entire work is given the date of the latest jokes.

One day in the future, a Columbia professor will be represented as having complained, in the nineteen-seventies, about a dull-witted Martian colleague's flimsy chronology. The Martian will have superseded a Californian in this account, but the Columbia historian's views about the problem will still be recoverable.

8.

In view of the inseparability of religion and peoplehood in Judaism, it may be worth while to subjoin a discussion on the child

---

[105] Genesis Rabba on 26.29; see my *Ancient Hebrew Fables*, 1973, p. 13. J. Levy, *Wörterbuch über die Talmudim und Midraschim*, 2nd ed., 1924, translates *qore'* in the fable by *Rebhuhn*, 'partridge', twice: in vol. 2, p. 476, s.v. *laghlegh*, and vol. 3, p. 220, s.v. *maqqora'*. (To which may be added J. Levy, *Wörterbuch über die Targumim*, 1867, p. 383, s.v. *qore'a, qora'a, qore'*.) However, in the principal entry of the word, vol. 4, p. 275, we are told that, while 'partridge' is its usual meaning, this fable employs it in the sense of *Rabe*, 'raven'—though the raven has no particularly long beak. The argument offered is that 'the well-known fable of the lion and raven is being recited'. There must be some lapse here.

of a Jewess and a gentile. Today it is considered Jewish, on virtually the same level as where both parents are Jews.[106] But the rule is post-Biblical, slowly evolving from the second century A.D. onwards and approaching victory only around A.D. 400. Behind it lies a sad tale of human tragedies—relieved by the compassionateness of the Rabbis.

We have seen[107] that, before the Babylonian exile, a gentile woman marrying a Jew automatically became a Jewess; accordingly, there was no problem about the offspring. From then on, however, a ritual of conversion was required, in the absence of which she was not deemed Jewish—and neither was the offspring. Ezra and Nehemiah saw to it that the new practice was strictly carried on after the return.

It is important to realize that the change did not affect the case of a Jewess marrying a gentile. Now as before she was lost to the nation. If anything, this would henceforth be insisted on more strongly: there was conscious determination to cut off one who went over to the heathen camp.

The finally prevailing canon by which we are now guided is found in no Tannaitic work. While a movement towards it is noticeable from the beginning of the second century A.D., in quite a few texts, Tannaitic and Amoraic, it is assumed that the child of a Jewess and a gentile is a gentile. In a number of others, it is classed as a bastard, *mamzer*. Evidently, the older standpoints were not definitely superseded till near the time of the redaction of the Talmud.

Before filling in details, it is advisable to dispose of an episode involving Herod Agrippa I—grandson of Herod the Great—which has been badly misconstrued.[108] Already his Edomite great-great-grandfather or great-great-great-grandfather had converted to Judaism. Nevertheless many people would resent a king not of pure lineage, and especially a descendant of Edomites who, even after conversion, were entitled to free intermarriage within Jewry only from the third generation on.[109] On a certain festival, when he was publicly reciting the paragraph of the king from Deuteronomy, on reaching the exhortation 'You may not put a foreigner over you

---

[106] See R. Posner, art. Jew, *Encyclopedia Judaica*, vol. 10, 1971, p. 23.
[107] See above, pp. 3 ff.
[108] Mishnah Sotah 7.8, Tosephta Sotah 7.16.
[109] Deuteronomy 23.8 f., as understood by the Rabbis: Mishnah Yebamoth 8.3.

who is not your brother',[110] he burst into tears. Whereupon the sages reassured him: 'Fear not, you are our brother'. In fact, they said 'you are our brother' three times, a formal acknowledgement.

Obviously, they were alluding to the provision concerning Edom just mentioned: 'You shall not abhor an Edomite, for he is your brother; the children of the third generation may enter into the assembly of the Lord'. Beyond this fact, not much can be said with confidence about their legal and political motives. R. Nathan of the second century A.D. charged them with sinful flattery. (According to Josephus, it is in order to flatter Herod the Great that the historian Nicolas of Damascus replaces his Edomite origin by a Babylonian Jewish one).[111] What is erroneous is the idea, entertained in modern literature,[112] that the report proves adherence as early as in Temple days to the principle that the child of a Jewess and a gentile is Jewish. It simply does not envisage a union of this nature. It is noteworthy that, however much the late Rabbis may have wished for a precedent from that date, nowhere in Talmud or Midrash do we meet this mix-up.

Now for some passages treating the offspring of a Jewess and a gentile as a gentile; and first, the Mishnic provision[113] that a proselyte with a Jewish mother may praise 'the God of our fathers'. No doubt this puts him above one with a gentile mother. Yet it still leaves him a proselyte. But for his conversion, that is, he would not be a Jew.

Similarly, the Bible tells us of 'the going forth of the son of an Israelite woman, who was the son of an Egyptian man, in the midst of the children of Israel'.[114] In Siphra,[115] the clause 'in the midst' and so on is declared 'to teach that he had converted to Judaism'. So a Jewish mother is not enough to make a man a Jew. Perhaps it should be added that the interpretation is unhistorical. The original narrator is not thinking of conversion; what he means is that the man, though sharing his father's status as a kind of resident alien,[116] went right among the full Israelites. Just so, Dinah 'went

---

[110] Deuteronomy 17.5. For the original point of this interdiction, see my article in *Journal of Biblical Literature*, vol. 90, 1971, pp. 480f.

[111] Josephus, *Jewish Antiquites* 14.1.3.9.

[112] See e.g. L. M. Epstein, *Marriage Laws in the Bible and Talmud*, 1942, p. 196.

[113] Mishnah Bikkurim 1.4.

[114] Leviticus 24.10.

[115] Siphra on Leviticus 24.10.

[116] See above, p. 5.

forth' among the full Shechemitesses.[117] For the present purpose, the difference is irrelevant: the point is that Siphra here no less than the Bible looks on the child of a Jewess and a gentile as a gentile.

Again, we hear of scholars of the third and fourth centuries allowing a proselyte with a Jewish mother to be a judge.[118] The breakthrough occurred when such a proselyte ran for town manager and his rival, an established scholar, demanded his exclusion before R. Joseph. The proselyte, however, had a Rabbinical friend, Adda bar Ahaba, who persuaded R. Joseph to lay down that a proselyte with a Jewish mother is 'from among your brethren'.[119] Joseph's pupil Raba adopted the opinion. By the way, the scholar was not left without comfort: a man like him, Joseph explained, had best devote himself to higher, 'heavenly' concerns, while the other one engaged in the more mundane city affairs. One is reminded of the division of labour between Mary and Martha envisaged by Jesus.[120]

It is not impossible that the case of the king-judge Agrippa I, though essentially quite different, plays a certain part: his distinguished Jewish ancestry on his mother's side was in his favour, a consideration which may conceivably have been generalised. At any rate, R. Joseph's verdict is a notable concession. Nevertheless, it definitely does treat the man as a proselyte, not as a native Jew. This is underlined by the reservation that a convert with a Jewish mother, even when installed as judge, may not act in questions respecting levirate marriage. Judgment here may determine a party's 'name in Israel',[121] and a proselyte comes from outside—even one whose mother is a Jewess.

According to the Acts of the Apostles,[122] Timothy had a Jewish-Christian mother and a Greek father. Paul, wishing to appoint him his assistant-missionary, circumcised him in deference to the Jews of the region, 'for they all knew that his father was a Greek'. The natural meaning is that they knew him to be a gentile: hence, if his mission was to have any chance with them, he had to be incorporated by circumcision.

---

[117] Genesis 34.1.
[118] Babylonian Yebamoth 102a, Qiddushin 76b.
[119] Deuteronomy 17.15.
[120] Luke 10.38ff.
[121] Deuteronomy 25.10.
[122] Acts 16.1ff.

Commentators, anachronistically carrying back into this period the principle that the child of a Jewess is always Jewish,[123] get into difficulties with 'for they all knew' and so on. What did it matter? One way out taken by some[124] is to regard Luke as ignorant of the Jewish position. But this is not a recondite, sophisticated detail. It is a matter as to which anybody with the remotest contact with Judaism would be informed. Another line attempted[125] is to postulate that the words in question are not to be taken in their natural sense. The Jews knew, Luke intends to convey, that Timothy, though one of them on account of his mother, was unlikely to be circumcised since his father was a gentile. However, why, if this is what Luke wants to say, he does not say it, remains unexplained. Also, it makes the Jews even worse jumpers to conclusions than they are. Had it been the law that such offspring was Jewish, it is difficult to see why circumcision on the eighth day should have been uncommon. Of Timothy, we know that he was very much brought up by his mother.[126]

Whether Paul, despite his rejection of proselyte circumcision, did in fact proceed as Luke relates, we need not decide; still less whether—within the framework of this tradition—he would have proceeded thus had both parents been gentiles. (I have little doubt that the account in Acts is true: his task takes precedence over consistency with doctrine. There are quite a few other examples.[127]) What matters in the present context is that the incident—historical or not—presupposes, indeed, is valuable evidence for, the old system under which a Jewess married to a gentile produces gentile progeny.

The earliest authority represented as deviating is Simeon of Teman, of the second century A.D., for whom the child was Jewish, though of the most inferior category: a bastard, *mamzer*. Within a very short time, Simeon ben Johai pronounced it legitimate, *kasher*.[128] The considered formulation of Mishnah,[129]

---

[123] Most of them rely on H. L. Strack and P. Billerbeck, *Kommentar zum Neuen Testament aus Talmud und Midrasch*, vol. 2, 1924, p. 741.

[124] See e.g. H. Conzelmann, *Die Apostelgeschichte*, 1963, p. 89.

[125] See e.g. E. Haenchen, *Die Apostelgeschichte*, 13th ed., 1961, p. 420, J. Munck, *The Acts of the Apostles*, 1967, p. 155.

[126] II Timothy 1.5.

[127] Some are quoted in my *Pauline Contributions*, pp. 227 ff.

[128] Palestinian Yebamoth 6b f., Qiddushin 64c f., Babylonian Yebamoth 16a f., 44ff., 99a, 102a, Qiddushin 68b, 75b ff., Abodah Zarah 59a.

[129] Mishnah Yebamoth 7.5.

Tosephta[130] and Siphra[131] opts for bastardy, though the Tosephta also notes the more generous line of Simeon ben Eleazar. Evidently, the portions in these sources presupposing that the child is a gentile are relics not brought up to date.

Among the followers of Simeon of Teman in the same century were Aqiba, Ishmael and Meir, in the third Johanan bar Nappaha, Hanina bar Hama, Ammi, Resh Laqish, Eleazar ben Pedath and Hiyya II bar Abba, and in the fourth Rabba bar Bar Hana and Dimi. Among the followers of Simeon ben Johai in the same century were Simeon ben Judah and Simeon ben Eleazar, in the third Bar Kappara, Jonathan ben Eleazar, Joshua ben Levi, Zeira and Mattena, in the fourth Rabin and in the fifth Rabina, Ameemar and Aha bar Raba. Judah the Prince and, it seems, Samuel too are variously assigned to one or the other faction.[132] My guess is that they in fact belonged to the former, being subsequently transferred to the latter as it was gaining in strength. As far as Judah the Prince is concerned, the Mishnah's official line—the child is a bastard—makes this a near-certainty. We shall find the same tendency at work in respect of Rab Judah bar Ezekiel and Raba.[133]

How did it come to recognition, be it as bastard, be it as legitimate? Nothing points to foreign inspiration. For one thing, in second-century Roman law, the offspring of a Roman woman married to an alien shared the latter's nationality.[134] It must be an internal development. But what accounts for it seeing that, in general, the Talmudic trend was towards ever greater strictness in this area? More particularly, what made it start in an age of extreme hostility to, and terrible suffering at the hands of, the occupying power? And why was the earliest advocate of full acceptance, legitimacy (at least the earliest named in the sources) Simeon ben Johai, a foremost opponent of assimilation and for years outlawed by the government?[135]

It is precisely the paradoxical aspect of the reform which furnishes the clue. In that fearful period, abuse of Jewish women by

---

[130] Tosephta Qiddushin 4.16.
[131] Siphra on Leviticus 22.13.
[132] Judah the Prince: Babylonian Yebamoth 45a; Samuel: Babylonian Yebamoth 45a, Palestinian Yebamoth 6c.
[133] See below, pp. 30 f.
[134] Gaius, Institutes 1.78, Ulpian, Regulae 5.8.
[135] How bitter he could be may be seen from Palestinian Qiddushin 66b.

the enemy was common. Significantly, the Talmud barely distinguishes between cruelties of this kind in Maccabean times and Hadrianic ones.[136] Rabbinical circles were not, of course, spared. The daughter of the martyred Hananiah ben Teradion was carried off to a brothel from where, we are told (with, perhaps, some embellishments), R. Meir, her brother-in-law, eventually bought her back.[137]

Imagine a place after a week's devastation by the soldateska. Here were pious wives and daughters of pious parents, raped. Suppose they gave birth to gentiles, that must cause not only much personal anguish but also, as the children grew up, tensions a critically enfeebled community could not afford. A reform of the traditional system was highly desirable. What made it possible was an integral element in the situation: the father against whom it was directed was absent, did not care one way or the other.

It may be asked why, if this is how the new regulation came about, it was carried on even when things became more peaceful. Part of the answer is that assault on women in one form or another never ceased being a real threat. We learn, for instance, of the ransoming towards the end of the third century of a Jewess who had become pregnant in captivity.[138] I do think, however, that the measure's chance of success would have been far less if it had not been sponsored by a man like Simeon ben Johai, generally the most adamant purist. (His stand against extradition of a fellow-Jew in any circumstances is typical.[139])

Simeon ben Teman held the child to be a bastard. From a modern point of view, his solution may look like having made matters worse. While a gentile can convert, thereby becoming more or less the equal of a born Jew, a bastard is virtually unable to rise, hence will never be a suitable marriage partner for an unblemished person. But this is not how they felt then. A bastard was at least one of them, inside, a Jew—and that was an immense improvement: it consoled the families afflicted and it averted the danger of rearing a fifth column. We should bear in mind that, during Hadrian's terror regime and often afterwards, the pagan authorities would make

---

[136] Babylonian Gittin 57b.
[137] Babylonian Abodah Zarah 18a f.
[138] Babylonian Yebamoth 45a.
[139] See my *Collaboration with Tyranny* in *Rabbinic Law*, 1965, pp. 28 ff., but also *Jewish Law Annual*, Suppl. 2, 1980, pp. 45, 59.

conversion a very risky affair. Anyhow, legitimacy began to replace bastardy quite soon.

Naturally, any measure giving relief in these heartbreak conditions had to be extended to marriage of a Jewess and a gentile. Most texts dealing with the topic employ a term which primarily designates an irregular union—a gentile 'comes upon', *ba' ʿal*, a Jewess[140]—which gives further support to my thesis. (Its first occurrence is in the complaint by Lot's elder daughter to the younger, after the destruction of Sodom, that 'there is no man on earth to come upon us'.[141]) The considered ruling of Mishnah and Siphra, however, speaks of a Jewess 'married to', *nisseʾth le*, a gentile.[142] Such a marriage might indeed be contracted in error as to his status: say, he gets circumcised but neither he nor his Jewish bride are aware that basptism is equally essential for conversion. I shall come back to this case[143] where, clearly, treatment of the offspring as Jewish would be called for on humanitarian and political grounds much as in the violent situations described above. Still, the new principle could not be applied selectively: it must cover any progeny of a Jewess.

A striking adumbration of the Rabbis' concessions regarding the status of offspring is contained in Paul's teaching, already adverted to,[144] about conversion of one of two spouses. As the convert is a new being, the marriage is ended; but if they stay together—which the apostle recommends—intercourse establishes a fresh marriage. This implies two momentous deviations from traditional practice: admission of marriage with a heathen and, since the fresh marriage comes about even where the convert is a woman, admission of a woman's capacity to 'consecrate', *qiddesh*, a man. Paul's argument for recognition is: 'else were your children unclean'.[145] True, the situation he deals with involves no violence; indeed, in a way, it is the opposite of that the Rabbis are facing. The latter, in response to the desperate losses suffered by their flock, try to mitigate such further disruption as they can. Paul's aim is to enhance the growth of an already growing Church. Yet, though coming from such dif-

---

[140] E.g. Tosephta Qiddushin 4.16.
[141] Genesis 19.31.
[142] Mishnah Yebamoth 7.5, Siphra on Leviticus 22.13.
[143] Babylonian Yebamoth 46a, cp. Palestinian Qiddushin 64c; see below, p. 30.
[144] See above, pp. 16 ff.
[145] I Corinthians 7.14.

ferent places—fear of utter ruin, hope for ever more glorious advance—or indeed, because of this, they are both led to basically the same concern.

Once the setting of the problem is seen, much that is otherwise puzzling falls into place. First, the enormous span of opinion: total exclusion of the child at one end, bastardy in the middle, legitimacy at the other end. Actually, it is even more extreme than might be thought: for the sponsors of the third, ultimately prevailing view, the child is legitimate—not a bastard—even if the mother is properly married to a Jew at the time.[146] If she had a child from another Jew, it would be a bastard. Surely, this dispensation could have originated only in the dire dilemma I am assuming. I am aware of the argumentation since built up so as to fit everything into a neat, logical structure.

Secondly, the long struggle between these various attitudes: some three hundred years. Even of as late an authority as Rabina, the Gemara finds it necessary to prove that he did not rank the child as a bastard.[147] This feature, too, is explained by the evolution here outlined, with rooted tenets being challenged by social exigencies. This usually makes for a tough conflict.

A third item is closely connected with the second: the ambivalence of quite a few sages confronted by the problem. Hiyya II, when visiting Gebal, nocited that Jewesses there married, and conceived from, gentiles who, having undergone circumcision, counted as proselytes though baptism had been omitted. He kept silent still ordered by his teacher Johanan to announce to them that their children were bastards.[148]

Also in the late third century, Judah bar Ezekiel counselled the son of a Jewess and a gentile either to marry 'a woman of his kind'—a bastard was permitted only to marry another bastard—or to conceal his antecedents so that he might marry into legitimate stock. Raba, in the fourth century, gave similar advice, to marry 'a woman of his kind' or go abroad.[149] The Gemara, to be sure, infers that these scholars deemed the questioner legitimate. They would not have suggested deceit for the purpose of wrongful marriage: they suggested it because a number of colleagues still stuck to the

---

[146] Babylonian Yebamoth 45b.
[147] Babylonian Qiddushin 68b.
[148] Babylonian Yebamoth 46a, Abodah Zarah 59a.
[149] Babylonian Yebamoth 45a.

less favourable judgment and, also, because even if their benign ruling was accepted, the man would not be welcome everywhere. However, this is most probably another instance of adherents to the stricter doctrine being re-classed.[150] Raba, as I pointed out,[151] at some stage or in some contexts at least, looked on such a person as not even a bastard but a gentile—as a proselyte if converted. The point is that the Rabbis were torn between time-hallowed principle on the one hand and gentleness and expediency on the other. I wonder whether, even in this century, it might not have been better in many cases if courts having to allow or disallow a marriage had asked fewer questions.

This is not to deny that, especially in the upper stratum of society, even with legitimacy granted, there would indeed be prejudice against admitting a person of inferior description into one's family. Rab,[152] approached by the son of a Jewess and a gentile, decided in favour of legitimacy, yet when the man asked him for his daughter's hand, declined. A younger confrère, Shimi bar Hiyya (elsewhere, too, in controversy with him),[153] quoted a proverb (in the manner of Rab[154]), 'In Shangri-la a camel will dance on a table',[155] adding: 'Here is the table, the camel and Shangri-la, but no dancing'. That is to say: your decision—he is legitimate—created a fairyland setting and we were all agog to watch the corresponding performance—his becoming your son-in-law—but it does not materialize. Rab retorted that he would not budge even if the suitor were like Moses's successor Joshua.[156] To which Shimi replied that, if he were like Joshua, he could easily find himself another wife despite Rab's rebuff; but as it was, other fathers would now be suspicious and reject him. As the man refused to leave, Rab fixed his eyes on him and he died.[157] (The sage was famous for his mastery of esoteric knowledge.[158] Earth from his grave was used to cure

---

[150] See above, p. 27.
[151] See above, p. 25.
[152] Babylonian Yebamoth 45a.
[153] E.g. Babylonian Berakoth 47a, Yoma 28b.
[154] E.g. Babylonian Sanhedrin 106a. See W. Bacher, *Die Agada der Babylonischen Amoräer*, 1878, p. 32.
[155] Literally, 'In Media, a camel dances on a *qab*'. A *qab* is about 2000 cubic centimeters.
[156] Cp. Babylonian Hullin 124a towards the end.
[157] Cp. Acts 5.5, 10.
[158] See W. Bacher, *op. cit.*, pp. 16ff.

fever.¹⁵⁹) He belonged to the aristocracy; and it may well be that daughter of his who subsequently married into the Exilarch's house.¹⁶⁰

Isaiah, according to legend,¹⁶¹ in a remotely comparable quandary, behaved differently from Rab. He had reproved King Hezekiah for remaining unmarried, and when the latter gave as his reason a vision that any children of his would be grave sinners, had rejected this as irrelevant: a man ought to do his duty and leave the rest to God. Hezekiah repented—and asked the prophet to let him have his daughter to wife. Isaiah agreed.

Incongruities in the determination of status are not unknown in modern systems. It so happened that, while I was sketching the foregoing history of the Jewish approach a few years ago, the International Social Service was fighting for some four thousand children born during the occupation of Japanese women married to Americans. Under present Japanese law they are aliens, and under American law their citizenship lapses unless they reside continuously for two years in the States between the ages of 14 and 28. No need to worry about a child of a Japanese woman and an American not married to one another: it is recognized as Japanese on the mother's entering it into the family register.

---

[159] Babylonian Sanhedrin 47b.
[160] Babylonian Hullin 92a.
[161] Babylonian Berakoth 10a; see my *Medical and Genetic Ethics: Three Historical Vignettes*, 1976, pp. 8ff.

EXCURSUS TO LECTURE I

The following material is culled from lectures and writings of mine in the period 1961-73. It may be of moderate interest even though much will be judged shallow or redundant now that we have available Calum Carmichael's chapter on Ruth in his great, I am tempted to say magical, book Women, Law and the Genesis Traditions.[1]

The book of Ruth is the Winter's Tale of the Bible: vain search for prosperity and fearful losses at first, mature reconciliation of the survivors and the promise of a new generation in the end. The family's head, Elimelech, 'God is King', and both his heirs, Mahlon and Qilyon, 'Sickly' and 'Weakly', die abroad, and one of his Moabite daughters-in-law, Orpah, 'the Turner-back', re-enters her native community. But the other, Ruth, 'the Friend', follows his widow, Naomi, 'the Pleasant one', to Elimelech's home at Bethlehem—though at this stage Naomi re-christens herself Marah, 'the Bitter-fated'; maybe there is here an echo of Tamar, who is cited in the Book as an old-time model for the two women and who also went through long years of suffering.[2] After a period of trial, they, joined by a relative of Elimelech's, Boaz, 'the Pillar'—a descendant of Judah and Tamar[3]—re-establish, and indeed ensure a glorious future for, the seemingly ruined house. (My translations of the names may not all stand up to scholarly etymology. What matters here is that they convey, I think, the narrator's understanding.) With a purposive and caring deity keeping watch, it is the loyalty, patience and wisdom of the protagonists that bring about the happy conclusion. Of Greek writers, Sophocles alone in his two dramas about Oedipus treats of the healing power of time in comparable fashion.[4]

---

[1] 1979, pp. 74 ff.
[2] Ruth 4.12, Genesis 38, on which latter episode see my The Duty of Procreation, 1977, pp. 4 f.
[3] Ruth 4.18 ff.
[4] See my article in *California Law Review*, vol. 68, 1980, p. 310. The role of time in Shakespeare's last plays is inspiringly discussed by Gustav Landauer, *Shakespeare*, 1922, vol. 2, pp. 240 ff., 280 ff. The work is among those edited by Martin Buber after the author's murder by right-wing extremists.

Arguably, we ought to speak of the Book of Naomi. The story begins with her, is dominated by her and terminates with her. It is she who emigrates with husband and sons, who returns solitary except for Ruth's devoted attendance and who is eventually recognized as, in an ultimate sense, the mother of the son born by the latter and destined to be the ancestor of King David. When the entire family is brought low, the Lord has testified 'against her', and when it prospers, to her the felicitations are tendered.[5] Every single step of Ruth is taken under her direction. By a curious coincidence, the road to expiation, peace and hope in the Winter's Tale is mapped out by one of the queen's friends not herself a participant in the main exchanges of love and hate.[6]

I shall occupy myself with a few facets to which, as a rule, it does not seem that justice is being done: the relation of youth and age (1), female friendship (2), the obstacle in the way of 'redemption' and the means of surmounting it suggested by Naomi (3), the following out of her design by Boaz (4), the counterpoint to the Book of Ruth supplied by that of Esther (5) and the nature of the Book (6).

1. Youth and age. To start with Boaz—he is fiftyish, about twice as old as Ruth. From their first encounter he addresses her as 'my daughter'.[7] He is 'a mighty man of wealth'.[8] His speech is dignified, almost solemn, his position and actions those of a respected, getting-on citizen. Though single, he engages in no amatory pursuits: obviously Naomi, when she encourages Ruth to visit him in the barn where he will lie down after a merry-making, is sure he will be alone.[9] As Ruth approaches him, offering to become his wife, he thanks her—'my daughter' again—for her kindness in not preferring somebody younger. No intercourse takes place: far from being an impetuous lover, he displays the utmost restraint. She suggestively occupies the place of a spouse—we must remember that, though by much his junior, she is a widow, not a trembling virgin. But that nothing happens beyond this is quite clear from his reflections on a kinsman with a better title who will have to be dealt with before they can go ahead. It would be too risky

---

[5] Ruth 1.21, 4.14 f.
[6] See G. Landauer, *op cit.*, p. 256.
[7] Ruth 2.8, 3.10 f.
[8] Ruth 2.1.
[9] Ruth 3.4.

to anticipate success in disposing of this prior claim. Indeed, Ruth leaves before dawn in order that their intimate meeting should not become public; otherwise suspicion would be aroused and they would be putting themselves very much in the wrong. A further, more specific motive for secrecy will emerge in due course. A little remark by Naomi provides corroboration. Having received Ruth's report, she assures her that they will not now have to wait long: 'the man will not sit still until he have finished the thing this day'.[10] There has been no fulfilment; but he is stirred. The shrewd lady knows the effect it will have—was it not all her doing?

It should be added that Tamar also conceived from a man belonging to the previous generation, Judah, her father-in-law. She also favoured him above a highly eligible younger option, his surviving third son. She also was far from inexperienced and threw herself in the boldest manner at the worthy to be won, as he was, like Boaz, alone after a festivity. Lastly, once enlightened as to where he stood, he, like Boaz, was fully capable of keeping his impulses in check.[11] Whether or not the earlier narrative finds the difference in age interesting, it would not escape the author of Ruth.

As for Naomi—her matronliness receives enormous emphasis and is in fact far more important than Boaz's seniority. As Ruth's mother-in-law, we would assume her to be roughly his contemporary. This may be checked. Her sons married while in Moab. Say, they were then around twenty, she around forty. We are told[12] that about ten years elapsed before they died and she returned—fiftyish. Two passages, however, add greatly to the picture. Early on, we learn in circumstantial language that she is virtually past childbearing;[13] and towards the close of the Book, her neighbours wish her joy because the babe 'will be a nourisher of your old age'[14]—the kind of felicitation suitable only for a woman with no more active aspirations.

2. Friendship. The Book has in common with a remarkable number of Old Testament plots involving succession that the major decisions are made by brave and resourceful women—even though, essentially, in behalf of their men who have to be trapped into their

---

[10] Ruth 3.18.
[11] Genesis 38.26.
[12] Ruth 1.4.
[13] Ruth 1.12 f.
[14] Ruth 4.15.

good fortune. Tamar, of course, comes to mind; Sarah, Rebekkah and Bathsheba are other examples.[15] But nowhere else do we find an attachment between two women as here, genuine, for better or worse, person to person. There is a trusting sharing of father-husband between Lot's daughters, deprived of any other human communication;[16] but it remains a single, if moving, episode. (Maybe there is a civilisatory dilution of a theme in the sequel: a child from the father for Lot's daughters, from the father-in-law for Tamar, from a senior kinsman for Ruth and Naomi.) Ruth accompanies Naomi into a country unknown to her, where they are likely to live in poverty and isolation. The latter in turn forgoes in favour of the former her own chances of gaining a 'redeemer', a new husband—at least as that role is normally understood. In deeper reality, as we shall see, theirs also is a sharing, though of a more refined sort than in the primeval legend, and just as in that legend, the elder one takes she initiative and lends encouragement to the younger one. Ruth 'loves' Naomi and to Naomi, who has lost her children, Ruth 'is better than seven sons'—as the barren Hannah's husband hopes to be to his wife.[17] The narrator takes pains to impress on us the extraordinary level attained by the two: Orpah aspired to it, at first intending, like Ruth, to journey with her mother-in-law, but finally she had not the courage. We must not forget that both Ruth and Orpah already in Moab chose an unusual path, by attaching themselves wholeheartedly to Judean refugees.[18] Ruth goes it to the end.

Actually, as far as I can make out, the alliance is unique in ancient literature. There are many parallels to David and Jonathan or Nisus and Euryalus,[19] male comrades risking their lives for one another. Stith Thompson contains dozens of such entries under Friendship[20]—not a single remotely corresponding one about women. The only approximation that occurs to me is in Sophocles: Ismene would like to die together with her sister Antigone. The relationship, however, is marred because, earlier on, she had not had the spirit to join Antigone in contravening the royal decree, so

---

[15] Genesis 21, 27, II Kings 1.
[16] Genesis 19.30 ff.
[17] Ruth 4.15, I Samuel 1.8 (ten sons).
[18] Ruth 1.8.
[19] Virgil, *Aeneid* 9.176 ff.
[20] *Motif-Index of Folk-Literature*, 1957, vol. 5, pp. 163 ff.

the latter now spurns her request. In a way, Orpah is reminiscent of Ismene.

Of the reasons for this lacuna in the sources it must suffice to name three, interconnected. One: our informants are mostly male, interested in women only insofar as their doings affect the male world. If any of Queen Vashti's ladies shared exile or the gallows with her,[21] we cannot expect to hear of it. (Not one dream of a Jewish woman is recorded by either the Old Testament or the New. A glance at Helen's Note-Books will reveal the icongruity of this.) Two: the heroic mode of mutual self-sacrifice popular with the bards—in battle, in political conspiracy—is on the whole outside the range of female activity. There is blood-brotherhood, no blood-sisterhood. Women serve in other ways. Three: to the extent that men mastered the art of *divide et impera*, an unbreakable bond between two women would in fact be a relatively rare achievement.[22] What a beautiful paradox. An extraordinary conflux of circumstances accounts for the commemoration of this pair. Yet it is Ruth's oath of allegiance to Naomi—'Whither you go I will go, the Lord do so to me if aught but death part you and me'[23]—that to this day is quoted as expressing the highest level of dedication, irrespective of sex; it figures in marriage celebrations; it has been set to music over and over again.

3. The marital problem: the scheme. Naomi, back at Bethlehem, is in control of what remains of Elimelech's realm, Ruth and the land. As regards the latter, this chimes with a pericope in the Second Book of Kings,[24] where a widow (with a son under age) resides on the estate, moves abroad during a famine, on her return finds herself dispossessed and is reinstated at the king's behest; she is even reimbursed for the fruits the intruders took in her absence.[25] Still, it is a sad existence: apart from the lack of a man, there is so little food that Ruth must procure some by gleaning. Boaz admires the high-minded couple, being particularly taken by Ruth—indeed, he says so to her.[26] Moreover, he appreciates their

---

[21] Esther 1; see below, p. 45.
[22] A reminder from modern times is furnished by Mörike's *Zwei Schwestern*, made into a duet by Brahms.
[23] Ruth 1.16 f.
[24] II Kings 8.1 ff.
[25] Cp. Digest 13.7.22.2, Ulpian XXX ad edictum: *A praedone enim fructus et vindicari extantes possunt et consumpti condici.*
[26] Ruth 2.11 ff.

need and makes it as easy as possible for them to get enough to eat from his fields. For all that, he is studiously cautious, takes no steps to accomplish a real change in their situation. He first meets Ruth at the beginning of the barley harvest: both it and the wheat harvest go by and he still is just supportive, tender—distant.

What more could he do? A great deal. If an impoverished owner of land has sold it or is about to sell it, his agnatic relations, in order of proximity, have the right, and a moral duty, to 'redeem' it, to buy it back or pre-empt it.[27] A clan's territory ought to be kept intact. Jeremiah, even while imprisoned by the authorities, 'redeems' a cousin's property, even while it is occupied by the Babylonian army.[28] Boaz could put it to Naomi that, should no closer relation come forward, he would be a generous purchaser. However, there is a snag. Under the system prevailing in this epoch, if the land belongs to a childless widow, a 'redeemer' must take her to wife and the firstborn will be her original husband's heir. In these special conditions, 'redemption' has strong affinity with levirate—best known from Tamar's romance. The Biblical levirate operates within the nuclear family, primarily where—as in the saga of Tamar—a married son dies childless in his father's lifetime: the widow, without change of family, goes to a brother and their firstborn will count as begotten by the deceased. (There is one extended application:[29] if, after the father's death, his sons stay together on the undivided estate[30] and one of them, married, dies childless, again, the widow is taken over by a brother and the first son ranks as the deceased's.) To be sure, the purpose of this institution is not to avert any loss of land but to provide a luckless family member with the line he hoped for.[31] Nevertheless, in the peculiar 'redemption' case involving a childless widow, once the agnate qualified steps forward, he must show the same concern for the deceased member of his clan—a very major point of contact. At any rate, this is what holds Boaz back: the requirement to marry the

---

[27] Leviticus 25.25 ff.

[28] Jeremiah 32.6 ff.

[29] Deuteronomy 25.5 ff. See my comments in *Juridical Review*, vol. 62, 1950, pp. 71 ff.

[30] Cp. Gaius, *Institutes* 3.154a: *Olim enim, mortuo patre familias, inter suos heredes quaedam erat legitima simul et naturalis societas quae appellabatur ercto non cito, id est dominio non diviso.*

[31] An arresting modern levirate, in James Purdy's Mourners Below, 1981, comes my way as this book is going into print.

dowager. It will soon become apparent that it is not a mere matter of carnal appetites—though I am the last person to pooh-pooh them.

Naomi has made up her mind that he would be the ideal protector. She is aware of his ground of hesitation. She also knows how to interpret his dealings with Ruth, reticent and tactful as they are. She decides to show him a way out of the impasse. She sends him Ruth, attired as for a wedding. He gets the message: he can do his duty by Naomi by taking charge of Ruth—who is very willing to fall in with the plan. At this juncture, there commences a phantasmagoria which will go on right to the finish, a series of scenes with the parties appearing in different masks and each mask itself being ambivalent. It is not, however, a play but a real-life struggle for high stakes. For the moment let us recall that Judah did his duty by Tamar, the respectable widow, by having intercourse with Tamar, posing—masked in the literal sense—as a whore. She thus, basically, acted both roles, of Naomi and of Ruth, at the same time. I cannot resist mentioning that the Winter's Tale culminates in a mummery (a sacred one, in a chapel[32]): the wronged queen is restored to her husband who has done penance for sixteen years, but first she is shown him as if she were a statue.

4. The marital problem: the execution. Boaz now is galvanized into action. He indicates to Naomi that he understands: while retaining Ruth as his bedfellow throughout the night—though without sexual commerce—in the morning he bids her take a bridal present, the *Morgengabe, pretium pudicitiae*, to Naomi.[33] In strict law, it is she who has been with him, as whose 'redeemer' he proceeds. The same day he sets out to tackle his potential rival, and the ingenuity by dint of which he eliminates him proves him worthy of being Naomi's choice. Before a quorum of elders, he asks him whether he whishes to 'redeem', purchase, Elimelech's land, up for sale; otherwise he, Boaz, will do so. The first answer, plainly anticipated, is yes. Then he goes on:[34] 'What day you buy the field from the hand of Naomi and from Ruth the Moabitess, you have bought the wife of the dead to raise up the name of the dead upon his inheritance'. The childless widow is part of the estate; and im-

---

[32] Mozart uses church music for the Count's pardon by the Countess in the last act of Le Nozze di Figaro.
[33] Ruth 3.15, 17. Cp. Genesis 24.22, 47, 53, 34.12.
[34] Ruth 4.5.

mediately the answer turns into no. The point is that Boaz, though by now he knows better, formulates in such a way that the other one can envisage only marriage with Naomi. Literally, 'the wife of the dead' may indeed describe either her or Ruth, both being childless widows; and this is of no small moment since Boaz must not be guilty of a straight falsehood. But as the phrase occurs in a statement about Elimelech's land, anyone trusting in fair play is bound to think of Naomi. Boaz himself had been alerted to the possibility of a substitution only the night before. We have to do with a mode of deception familiar from the Jacob cycle, for instance.[35]

The transaction is so not comprehended by most scholars that they revise the text in order to get rid of the ambiguity: 'What day you buy the field from the hand of Naomi, you have bought Ruth the Moabitess, the wife of the dead'.[36] Ruining everything—like many an emendation.[37] It destroys the artful web woven by the three heroes in cooperation; it represents Boaz as leaving the outcome entirely to chance, or worse, to his opponent's discretion; and it makes the latter's emphatic refusal most uncomplimentary to Ruth. It is indeed possible that the words 'and from Ruth the Moabitess' are an interpolation, dating from a time when the figure of Naomi lost in prominence and the subtleties of the plot began to be less fully grasped. They are not included in Boaz's final declaration of 'redemption'.[38] Be this as it may, on no account should we tamper with the deliberately misleading concentration on marriage with Naomi. The dangerous candidate withdraws because that is not what he wants—just as Boaz had not wanted it.

All this is illumined by the reason he gives, 'lest I spoil my own inheritance'.[39] No passage in this work has produced more headaches. How could 'redemption' marriage—whether with Naomi or with Ruth—interfere with his own patrimony? The firstborn would obtain Elimelech's, but nothing else, nothing from his physical begetter. What does he fear? Commentators mostly resort to evasion.[40] The very replacement of the forceful 'to spoil',

[35] See my Studies in *Biblical Law*, 1947, repr. 1969, pp. 191 ff.
[36] See e.g. E. Würthwein, *Ruth*, in *Die Fünf Megilloth, Handbuch zum Alten Testament*, vol. 18, 1969, pp. 19 f.
[37] E.g. the treatment of $^{\circ}o$ *nishba* as a dittography of $^{\circ}o$ *nishbar* in Exodus 22.9.
[38] Ruth 4.9.
[39] Ruth 4.6.
[40] Here is a desperate non-lawyer's projection: 'The storyteller, of course, was not interested in the legal points'. L. P. Smith, *The Book of Ruth*, in *The Interpreter's Bible*, vol. 2, 1953, p. 849.

'to destroy', 'to wipe out', by a vague 'to mar' in English versions is revealing. Well, the explanation is that he has Naomi in mind, unlikely to have any more children. So for a few years' enjoyment of Elimelech's riches, he would leave his own heirless. But could he not marry a younger woman in addition? No. It is evidently assumed that he cannot. Which means either that the events take place in an interregnum of monogamy—not unimaginable—or, at least, that where it is your duty to see to the revival of a dead relation's name, you may not take another wife before you have satisfied it. Near Eastern documents offer several cases in which no second wife is allowed; and Jacob binds himself by treaty to refrain from further conquests.[41] Considering that both Tamar's story and an extensive regulation in Deuteronomy dwell on the faithlessness of levirs,[42] it will not be surprising if the law debars a 'redeemer' of a childless widow's estate from similar conduct. The temptation to play false would be gigantic. It is relevant to note that Deuteronomy itself, while admitting that a delinquent levir may perpetuate his own name, makes the perpetuation worthless: the name will be tained for ever.[43]

Boaz, I maintained above, was unenthusiastic about marriage with Naomi from motives transcending sex-appeal. It can now be said that he, too, dreaded the extinction of his own name. This does not, it should be stressed, put him on the same level: his sustained solicitude for the two returnees testifies to his dependable, unselfish side. Again, I hinted at a specific object of his in not permitting Ruth's nocturnal call to transpire. This also is now clear. Had it become known, his competitor might well have sensed that a stratagem was afoot, perhaps even guessed its drift. As it is, he is thoroughly fooled. It should be observed, however, that even when he has expressed his disinterest, the circumspect, steady Boaz does not immediately come out with the truth. If he did that, the other one would change his mind and, especially since he has been tricked, would have little difficulty in getting an informal refusal held void. Hence Boaz calmly waits till the surrender of title is ratified by a solemnity that puts it above any attack, renders it ab-

---

[41] Genesis 31.50. See R. Yaron, *Introduction to the Law of the Aramaic Papyri*, 1961, p. 60.
[42] Genesis 38, Deuteronomy 25.5 ff.
[43] Deuteronomy 25.10.

solute, 'confirms' it.⁴⁴ (Jacob's extraction of an oath after Esau has already informally ceded his birthright is analogous.⁴⁵) It is only then that he triumphantly announces: 'You are witnesses that I have bought all that was Elimelech's and Qilyon's and Mahlon's. Moreover—the climax—Ruth the Moabitess, wife of Mahlon, have I bought to be my wife, to raise up the name of the dead upon his inheritance'. So Ruth the desirable, thirty-year-old, fertile one is 'the wife of the dead' whom the nearer kinsman renounced. Boaz, not at all a passive recipient of good luck, has skilfully carried out the operation the women entrusted to him. The ancient audience of the epic would share their happiness and laugh at their victim.

The Tamar precedent plays a considerable part in this scene at the city gate. The rival 'will not spoil' his own domain for the sake of the dead Elimelech. Onan 'spoilt' his semen in order not to lose a portion of the patrimony for the sake of his dead brother.⁴⁶ The moral: in a sense, here is a repetition of Onan's betrayal, this kinsman, too, withholds his semen from the bereaved widow. Yet it is not a simple identification. With superb craftsmanship we are given to understand that, blind as he is, he 'spoils' precisely while intent on 'not spoiling'. There is more. Under the Deuteronomic ordinance already adverted to, one who, roughly speaking, acts like Onan is publicly shamed: he has his shoe taken off by the woman he abandons in front of the elders.⁴⁷ The potential contender, by way of releasing his lien, in front of the elders takes his shoe off himself.⁴⁸ True, he does so in compliance with a ritual customary for certain major transactions. But, surely, the author wishes us to see him at the same time as a dupe, suffering self-inflicted disgrace. Yet a further allusion should be listed. Onan is killed by God. So, on a certain level, is the outwitted relative. While Judah and Boaz are among the ancestors of David, he is forgotten by history. This

---

⁴⁴ Ruth 4.7, *qiyyem*; *negotium conficere* in Cicero's terminology—see next footnote.
⁴⁵ Genesis 25.33; see my *Studies in Biblical Law*, p. 196. Cicero, *De Officiis* 3.14.58 f., tells of the owner of a lakeshore villa who, while entertaining a prospective buyer, got a large number of retainers to row about pretending to be catching fish. The guest offered a high price. But a simple, informal sale would not have been good enough since in the resultant *bonae fidei* proceedings the judge would take account of fraud. Accordingly, the vendor got his visitor to confirm the sale by a formal 'literal contract', leading to strict proceedings with, at that time, no allowance for misrepresentation.
⁴⁶ Ruth 4.6, *hishhith*, Hiphil, Genesis 38.9, *shiheth*, Piel.
⁴⁷ See my article in *Orita*, vol. 3, 1969, pp. 35 f.
⁴⁸ Ruth 4.2 ff.

is brought out dramatically by the fact that, in contrast to the other persons who have speaking names, names indicating their character and destiny, he has no name whatever. Boaz addresses him as 'such a one',[49] a unique usage in Scripture. His greed did him no good. It made him obtuse, and for the things temporal he lost the things eternal.

The dazzling alternation of roles goes on after his defeat. Boaz marries Ruth and the people hope his house will be blessed like that of Pharez, the offspring of Judah and Tamar. Yet when, in due course, they have a son, it is Naomi who receives congratulations on successful 'redemption', who formally takes up the heir and places him in her lap, and whose neighbours exclaim, 'There is a son born to Naomi', and call him Obed, 'Servant (of God)', doubtless in memory of Elimelech, 'God is King'.[50] Here we must remind ourselves that several wives of patriarchs, when unable to conceive, lent female slaves or quasi-slaves of theirs to their husbands, with a view to the progeny being credited to them.[51] It is manifestly this arrangement on which that devised by Naomi is patterned. In legal construction, through Ruth, she is vicariously cohabiting with Boaz. And inevitably, just as in the tales about the patriarchs, there is a constant to and fro between construction and material actuality. The latter prevails in the genealogy appended in the last four verses of the last chapter: Obed here figures as Boaz's son, not Elimelech's.

5. Esther. From the foregoing discussion, it is certain that there is in Ruth a persistent harking back to the Tamar incident. In turn, as I have set out elsewhere,[52] the Book has helped to shape the account of the Feeding of the Multitude in all four gospels and that of the Annunciation in Luke. The question I would raise now is whether it has influenced Esther.

If, with Goethe, we dub the Book of Ruth the loveliest idyll coming down from antiquity, that of Esther is definitely the greatest thriller. I know of no work Eastern, Greek or Roman rivalling it as to construction, tension, flow of events, denouement. How such a perfect specimen of its genre came to be produced we shall probably never find out.

---

[49] Ruth 4.1.
[50] Ruth 4.12 ff.
[51] Genesis 16.2, 30.2, 9.
[52] See my *The New Testament and Rabbinic Judaism*, 1956, repr. 1973, pp. 27 ff.

In Ruth, salvation is wrought by a foreign woman being brought in, in Esther, by a Jewish woman being sent out. Both selflessly leave their native base. But Ruth, of Moabite provenance, is to become an ancestress of David, Esther, related to the family of Saul, relinquishes any hope of being a link in her people's continuation. In Biblical times, a child's nationality follows the father's. When Mordecai tells her that, if she dissociates herself from the beleaguered Jewish community, it will be rescued in some other way but 'she and her father's house will perish',[53] the warning carries an overtone of pathos: her glory cannot be transmitted to any descendants. Significantly, whereas generally in the Old Testament motherhood or barrenness is recorded in respect of far lesser figures, here not a word. The silence is deafening: whether or not she had children does not matter. Buber somewhere admires Abraham for offering up on mount Moriah not just the present but hope. Esther, and also Mordecai, her adoptive father, otherwise progenyless, are equally devout and there is no angel from heaven intervening at the last moment. The tragic component of this tale is tremendous. (We should assign to it also the court-Jew quality of Mordecai's and Esther's final position.[54]) They do, of course, by their sacrifice deliver Jewry—and the world. German-Jewish orthodoxy, in whose midst I grew up, despised anyone marrying out—but far less if the gentile partner was high-placed. (Other sins too were rendered more venial by success: Heine and Disraeli could be mentioned.) This was not, as I then thought, sheer worship of the golden calf or the like. There was also the feeling that important well-wishers outside were badly needed for the embattled minority's survival. The exemplar of Esther might have been a consolation to many a traditionalist family with a straying member.

The Book of Ruth, I said above, might be entitled the Book of Naomi. Just so, the Book of Esther might be entitled the Book of Mordecai. He is introduced at the beginning of the main part, he plans the decisive steps and he receives the final eulogy. Instead of a woman, however, there is a man at the helm. This drama is set in a milieu of machismo. In its defence, the court indeed resorts to

---

[53] Esther 4.14.
[54] See my *Typologie im Werk des Flavius Josephus*, no. 6 of *Sitzungsberichte der Bayerischen Akademie der Wissenschaften*, Phil.-Hist. Klasse, 1977, pp. 24 ff., English translation in *Journal of Jewish Studies*, vol. 21, 1980, pp. 33 ff.

strong measures;[55] and it is the banishment of proud Queen Vashti in the opening scene which makes possible Esther's rise—a bit as the extinction of Naomi's closest ones except Ruth makes possible the latter's union with Boaz. Not surprisingly, insistence on male supremacy in Esther does not render female charms and ruses any less effective than they are in Ruth.

Both heroines are bereft of parents, yet both are granted wonderful replacement. Ruth adopts Naomi as her mother—though the term 'to foster', 'to rear', which one might expect, is reserved for the finale where Naomi becomes the adoptive mother of Ruth's son.[56] Mordecai adopts Esther as his daughter and 'fosters' her.[57] Both heroines must undertake dubious, risky enterprises, requiring perseverance at once and boldness at the right moment; and both scrupulously obey their respective guides.[58] Naomi advises Ruth how to enhance her attractiveness for Boaz,[59] Mordecai enquires every day as Esther is being prepared for her first meeting with the King.[60] In both recitals, the turning point from peril to deliverance occurs at night.[61] At a time of distress, Naomi calls herself 'the Bitter one',[62] and Mordecai 'cries with a loud and bitter cry'.[63] What Naomi seeks for her widowed daughters-in-law is 'rest'; at first she recommends they find it through re-marriage in Moab, afterwards she procures it, perfectly, for Ruth.[64] Haman urges the King 'not to let the Jews rest' but in the end, having triumphed, 'they rest from their enemies'.[65]

In both Books, there is much disguise and ambiguity. I have dwelled sufficiently on the masks in Ruth; Esther's concealment of her roots is, of course, crucial. As for utterances inviting misinterpretation, Elimelech's nearest agnate thinks, reasonably but wrongly, that the 'widow of the dead' offered in marriage is Naomi; by declining, he loses out and enables Boaz to win. Haman thinks,

---

[55] Esther 1.16 ff.
[56] Ruth 4.16.
[57] Esther 2.7, 20.
[58] Ruth 3.5, Esther 2.10, 20.
[59] Ruth 3.3.
[60] Esther 2.11.
[61] Ruth 2.8 ff., Esther 6.1 ff.
[62] Ruth 1.20.
[63] Esther 4.1.
[64] Ruth 1.9, 3.1.
[65] Esther 3.8, 9.16, 17, 18, 22.

reasonably but wrongly, that he is the man for whom the King devises a special honour; by counselling on this basis, he brings about humiliation for himself, aggrandisement for Mordecai.[66] The element of literalism noticeable in these cases comes into full play in connection with the edicts determining the fate of Jewry. The first one allows the populace to crush it out. A royal edict cannot be revoked. So the second one, in substance a revocation, is worded as an encouragement of the intended victims to arm themselves and resist. With the result that it is their assailants who are decimated.[67]

In all likelihood, none of these agreements and disagreements is due to contact. Nevertheless, the following line may be defensible.

The Book of Esther has been explained as, essentially, a heathen myth—be it in celebration of spring, be it in celebration of the victory of the Babylonian gods Ishtar and Marduk over Elam. It has been explained as referring to a historical persecution, under one regime or another. It has been explained as an allegory of wisdom in action. I suspect there is truth in all these theories: the story has gone through many stages. I have myself contributed yet a further twist: the final editor presents a political program, impressing on a government which hosts Jews that the proper course is not to annihilate them but to profit by their commercial and diplomatic skills.[68] Such an accumulation of layers is far from unique. Think of the road from Hero and Leander via Romeo and Juliet to West Side Story. Just conceivably, one of those through whose hands the work passed was acquainted with Ruth and touched up some passages so as to evoke that precedent. If I had to single out one instance—to Naomi's daring proposal that Ruth visit Boaz at night, the latter replies: 'All that you say I will do'. Then she does go 'according to all that her mother-in-law bade her'. As Esther is taken to the palace among the candidates for queenship, she daringly keeps silent as to her origin, 'for Mordecai had bidden her not to reveal it'; and once again, as she wins the crown, we are told of her silence 'as Mordecai had bidden her, for she did the saying of Mordecai, since he was fostering her'.[69] Admittedly, reiteration of striking points is a characteristic of Esther, so we must not make too much of this aspect of the parallel; it is pretty impressive anyhow.

---

[66] Ruth 4.5 ff., Esther 6.6 ff.
[67] Esther 8.8 ff.
[68] See *Jewish Quarterly Review*, vol. 37, 1946, pp. 139 ff.
[69] Ruth 3.5 f., Esther 2.10, 20.

6. Nature of the work. That Ruth conveys profound messages in a number of areas—religious, moral, social, political, international—is universally recognized. What has not been ventilated is the possibility that, in addition to other aims, it advocates a legal reform, is a *Rechtslegende* like, say, the account of the rescue of Susannah.[70] This virtuous woman, we read, was sentenced to death after two elders had testified against her in the traditional, collective manner; but when, at an inspired young sage's instance, they were examined in one another's absence, their contradictions proved her innocent. It has long been seen that a major purpose of this story is to secure acceptance of the up-to-date Pharisaic method of hearing witnesses. I have little doubt that, similarly, the Book of Ruth intends to recommend a relaxation in the province of 'redemption': there is to be an acknowledged proviso that, should the childless widow owner be above a certain age, a junior dependent may be substituted.

We should remember that complications of this kind were then quite important. By the Talmudic era, 'redemption' had long been theoretical, so a large amount of ancient detail has dropped out. But comparable problems affecting the levirate are indeed debated in considerable depth. In the matter of virility, for example, a distinction is drawn between a man congenitally impotent and one impotent in consequence of castration or old age: the former is totally excluded from this marriage, the latter is not, in principle, but even he must avoid it by extending the refusal which Deuteronomy, thinking of a healthy levir, treats as unforgivable[71]—all of it mitigating the rigour of the law.

However, I shall not enlarge. This excursus is too long already. I am reminded of an occasion ages ago, when I delivered a lecture before the Cambridge University Jewish Society and the then Chief Rabbi was asked to open the discussion. He spoke longer than I, there was no time for any further input and the student-President immediately rose to propose the vote of thanks. That cheeky guy thanked the Chief Rabbi for his address, introduced by Dr. Daube.

---

[70] See my remarks in *Revue Internationale des Droits de l'Antiquité*, vol. 2, 1949, pp. 200 f., and *Jewish Journal of Sociology*, vol. 3, 1961, pp. 12 ff.
[71] Tosephta Yebamoth 2.6.

LECTURE II

ERROR AND IGNORANCE AS EXCUSES IN CRIME

1.

Modern law in general negates criminality if your action would be alright had the facts been as you supposed they were: it is not theft if I take your purse thinking it to be mine. Several of the principal American decisions[1] date from 1860-80. A police officer arrests somebody he mistakenly considers drunk. (One is reminded of an incident some three thousand years ago, when the high priest Eli wrongly reproved Hannah, mother of Samuel.[2]) A railroad conductor forcibly ejects a passenger of whom he falsely assumes that he did not pay his fare: he has not committed assault and battery. A householder aims at and injures a member of a crowd who, engaged in shooting for a lark, seem to be attacking his residence. A man believes a girl's lie that she is eighteen[3] and takes her with him: this is not abduction. I omit detailed reservations such as that the mistake must be honest and reasonable or that, even in the absence of criminal liability, there may be a civil tort, negligence and so on. The main point is that, basically, these cases are not treated as crimes.

The very earliest courts do not admit such exemption. The most famous illustration of the theme is Oedipus who killed his father and married his mother, not knowing who they were. To be sure, his story does not fall within the legal sphere proper, but it does suggest that, initially, a tribunal would make no allowance for moral innocence. Confirmation is furnished by the very gradual way—to be inspected presently—in which ancient legislators loosen rigid accountability.

It is still a popular inference among historians and anthropologists that the 'primitives' could not grasp and, indeed, were not troubled by the problem: they 'did not distinguish', it is

---

[1] See R. M. Perkins, *Criminal Law*, 2nd ed., 1969, pp. 820, 939.
[2] I Samuel 1.13 ff.
[3] See R. Cross, *Law Quarterly Review*, vol. 91, 1975, p. 553.

claimed, 'between causation and fault'.⁴ So astute a psychologist as E. R. Dodds holds Athens as late as in the fifth century to be 'a society which judged men by their actions, not by their intentions'.⁵ But the mere fact that incidents involving this complication are so amply and carefully recorded points up the fallacy of the doctrine. There is actually no period in antiquity accessible to us when error and ignorance were not comprehended as fully as today. Why, then, does the oldest law not cater for them?

Three reasons may be mentioned. First, what I would call submission to fate. If you upset the order of things, then, however free of guilt in the subjective sense—whether by reason of mistake or because it was a sheer accident—you have done it. To be moved by and pay heed to this crude given must strike many rationalist ethicists as indefensible; but, whether it is or not, it by no means implies obtuseness to the plight of the actor. Few people even today disregard the objective entirely. If you at night fire into branches near your window where you think a burglar or rapist is lurking and the dead turns out to be your child who had been building a tree-house, very likely you will reproach yourself for a long while; similarly, if a friend of yours to whom you show your new gun is hit owing to malfunction. 'Leonore, forgive', Fiesko entreats his wife whom he has slain: she had disguised herself too successfully as the despicable tyrant Gianettino Doria.⁶ Therapists are busy with mothers of thalidomide babies or of daughters developing cancer as a result of fertility pills the mothers were given.

I cannot help feeling that exclusive attention to the inner is bloodless. I remember a discussion with a leading classicist. I put it to him that it was understandable if a mother whose kid was run over by a motorist, however blameless, might not want to see him socially. He replied that he would have nothing to do with such a woman. This is surely over-intellectual; and passing strange coming from an expositor of Greek tragedy. On the other hand, the literalistic attitude of another eminent Oxonian is no better. A schoolmistress teaching in the city rented a farmhouse in a

---

⁴ See R. Maschke, *Die Willenslehre im Griechischen Recht*, 1926, p. 60: *eine Auffassung, die zwischen Kausalität und Verschuldung noch nicht unterschied*. My brother Benjamin Daube accepts this view in *Zu den Rechtsproblemen in Aischylos' Agamemnon*, 1938, p. 186.

⁵ See E. R. Dodds, *Plato, Gorgias*, 1959, p. 218.

⁶ Schiller, *Die Verschwörung des Fiesko zu Genua*, Act 5, Scene 13.

neighbouring village. As the daily travel proved too much, she moved to the city and sublet the house, minus one room for an occasional visit. When her tenants turned out, to her horror, to have indulged in marijuana, she was hauled to court under an Act rendering punishable 'a person concerned in the management of premises used for the purpose of smoking cannabis or dealing in cannabis'—language taken over from older measures for the suppression of opium dens. My interlocutor held she should incur the rigour of the statute which imposed its penalty on her situation, without requiring a culpable state of mind: she was concerned in the management—enough. He shared none of my repugnance to the extreme injustice she would be suffering, declaring that this was no reason for not applying the law: life was often unjust. By an amusing coincidence, it was another, more human member of All Souls, Richard Wilberforce, who, when the case came before the Lords, supported the ruling in her favour.[7]

When, in course of time, ancient systems do relieve mistake and accident from the regular reprisals, they nonetheless often retain some purging to be undergone. Oedipus, even at the advanced stage where his alibi is accepted, needs purification. The Old Testament prescribes sacrifices for sins committed unknowingly,[8] and the unwitting homicide is relegated, temporarily at least, to a city of refuge.[9] Exculpation does not entail radical dismissal of actuality.

It may be worth while in this connection to advert to the psychoanalytical finding that, frequently, mistake or accident constitutes a less than total dissociation of the actor's soul from the act.[10] When I take your purse believing it to be mine, or when my revolver goes off while I show it to you, though at first sight the imbroglio appears to be entirely against my will, on deeper probing a resentment buried deep down in me may emerge as having contributed. No doubt this line of approach can be overdone. Milo Bosic makes use of it in The Judge, but it feels a bit forced.[11] Still, an adumbration occurs as early as in a story about Abraham and Sarah.[12] They conceal their marital relationship from the King of

---

[7] Sweet v. Parsley [1970], *Appeal Cases*, pp. 159 ff.
[8] Leviticus 4 f.
[9] Numbers 35, Joshua 20.
[10] See below, p. 66: *tout condamner*.
[11] On the problem treated by him, see my *Collaboration with Tyranny in Rabbinic Law*, 1965, E. J. Schochet, *A Responsum of Surrender*, 1973..
[12] Genesis 20.

Gerar. So he takes her into his harem but, as he is pure in heart, God prevents him from touching her. Strictly, it follows that, had he indeed had intercourse, he could not have been without some evil intent, however vague, diffuse, covered up.

The dilemma between inner and outer, of course, arises not only where the order is breached without *mens rea* but also in the converse case, where a person does act with *mens rea* but the breach fails to materialize, wholly or partially. In the Marriage of Figaro, the Count spends a pleasurable hour in the park at night with his wife, believing himself to be adulterously in the arms of the servant girl with whom he is in love. Similarly, in a post-Mozartian, bowdlerized version of Così Fan Tutte, the two heroines are unfaithful, not each with the other's fiancé, but each with her own who masquerades as a stranger.[13] There are comparable episodes in many literatures,[14] starting with the patriarchs. The lady Jacob's son Judah takes for a harlot is really his widowed, childless daughter-in-law, and an ancestor of King David results from this encounter.[15] Josephus[16] tells of a prominent Jew who, smitten with the charms of one of the Egyptian king's dancing-girls, was laying plans to approach her—a very risky enterprise. His brother, pretending to be helpful, dressed up his beautiful young daughter in a tutu, and the infatuated fellow was happily duped. From this marriage, too, came an extraordinary son.

Plato[17] discusses a variety of *mens rea* with lucky ending that corresponds more to accident: you smite somebody with murderous intent but somehow do not manage to finish him off. Our attempt.[18] The philosopher is emphatic that, morally, you are a slayer. Yet in deference to your fortune and genius, your penalty must be scaled down. This is my point, acknowledgement of the outcome, and he advocates a balance between it and the subjective posture.

A second element in the passivity of archaic procedure vis-à-vis mistake is the, to this day, troublesome conundrum of delimitation:

---

[13] See E. Newman, *More Stories of Famous Operas*, 1943, p. 222.

[14] See Stith Thompson, *Motif-Index of Folk-Literature*, 1957, vol. 4, J-K, pp. 432, 443.

[15] Genesis 38.14 ff.; see above, p. 39.

[16] Josephus, *Jewish Antiquities* 12.4.6.186 ff.

[17] Plato, *Laws* 9.876E f.; see my *Forms of Roman Legislation*, 1956, repr. 1979, pp. 79 f.

[18] Cp. e.g. G. Williams, *Criminal Law*, General Part, 2nd ed., 1961, pp. 136 f., 654.

which kind should exonerate and which should not? The Amalekite who gave the coup de grâce to Saul and the assassins of his son Ishbosheth were hoping for a reward from David. Instead, he had the former executed as a regicide, the latter as common murderers.[19] Perhaps, they were not at all wrong in thinking that their actions were agreeable to the man they benefited. But if so, he would not admit it—maybe not even to himself. We have to consider also that whoever is in power—as David by now was—has an enormous interest in the principle of unconditional inviolability: to accept any explanations from these adventurers would have set a dangerous precedent. (Just so, in trials after an 'illegitimate' regime is toppled, one reason for the extensive admission of the defence of superior orders is that the present, 'legitimate' regime wants its own orders obeyed without scrutiny: in the absence of that defence, people would have to ask themselves whether what they were bidden to do might not get them into trouble should there be another reversal.[20]) So it was killings under a misapprehension. What would be their status in modern theory? Are we consistent in our response to security organs overstepping their functions in misguided zeal?

Or take the assembly that sentenced Susannah to death. Daniel's intervention saved her, but we cannot expect a prophet to appear every time there is a miscarriage of justice. Nowadays judges are not answerable for their slips; but this canon is hardly self-evident.

The chief reason, however, is the third one: the difficulty of proof. In a loose-knit society, without means of easy communication, without police, without machinery for checking allegations of data that are not obvious, it is precarious to allow for exceptions. Though it is realized that they occur, there is virtually no hope of establishing one with certainty.

To appreciate the relevance of this aspect, we must remember also the relation between central authority and family in this epoch. The former, still very weak, is trying hard to dissuade the latter from self-help. If the impression were created that a slayer, a burglar, an adulterer could easily get off in court by a special plea, people would be even more reluctant to forgo private vengeance

---

[19] II Samuel 1.5 ff., 4.2 ff.
[20] See my *The Defence of Superior Orders*, 1956, p. 16, repr. in *Law Quarterly Review*, vol. 72, 1956, p. 507.

than they are anyhow. This policy on the part of the state of paying for major gains by minor, if alluring, concessions seems quite common. When Deuteronomy imposes capital punishment on an unfaithful wife or an obstreperous son, the harshness is in part at least designed to placate the diehards who would otherwise hold on to *iudicium domesticum*.[21] Once the public monopoly is assured, things can be more relaxed.

Present-day law, while attaching weight to mistake of fact, by and large still sticks to the maxim *ignorantia iuris non excusat*. Our judges, to be sure, are no more accountable for legal misconceptions than factual ones: but I cannot here explore this fascinating tenet.

Once again, the most quoted paradigms belong to 1860-80.[22] You injure somebody, incorrectly supposing you are entitled to do so in order to protect your property; maladvised by your counsel, you act in a manner that constitutes tax fraud; being an alien newly arrived, you contravene a precept unheard of in your country. Your mistake of law does not exonerate you. Of the arguments offered in juristic literature, the most serious one is that abandonment of this principle would open the door to pretence: many an accused who knew the rules perfectly well would be tempted to deny it.[23] There is some truth in this. Only it is remarkable that, as soon as they turn to remoter ages, scholars rarely think of such considerations as having played any part. When the 'primitives' do without the defense of mistake, with regard to law or fact, it must be stupidity.

Presumably, besides the awkwardness of proof, the two other factors noted above, respect for fate and elusive delimitation, are relevant in the area of ignorance of law too. There is, of course, enormous significance in this type being treated unsympathetically so much longer than mistake of fact. No doubt, one element is the inclination to see the norms in force as so natural that truly genuine error or ignorance is precluded. At the same time, insofar as it is admitted to be genuine, it is apt to be a sign of deviance—not readily tolerated. This brings us to what may be most important: a clinging to the sacrosanctity of the legal edifice, threatened if it were admitted that a mistake about it, however much beyond your con-

---

[21] See my discussion in *Juridical Review*, vol. 90 (n.s. 23), 1978, pp. 177 ff.
[22] See R. M. Perkins, *op. cit.*, pp. 920 ff.
[23] See R. M. Perkins, *op. cit.*, p. 925.

trol, will let you off. It is au fond the same instinct to uphold the structure which helps to keep Socrates from running away from his punishment though previously he flouted quite a few objectionable decrees.[24]

Here I would say a word about violations of sacred barriers, taboos. In this domain, as is well known, inner blamelessness is particularly slow in becoming a guarantee against requital. Neither Teiresias nor Actaeon, approaching a fountain for a drink, expects to come upon Athena or Artemis bathing; none the less both incur grievous chastisement for the forbidden sight.[25] In preparation for God's descent on Sinai, any touching of the mount is prohibited on pain of death—and the threat includes even beasts.[26] As the Philistines return the captured Ark of the Covenant to the Israelites, some of the latter joyfully gaze on it—and pay with their lives.[27] Again, King David hopes to bring it to Jerusalem and, at a certain moment during the operation, it would topple were it not for one Uzzah holding it up: he is struck down there and then.[28] The sketchiest account of what makes for this strictness would take us far beyond the present topic, which is the ordinary criminal law. It must suffice to point out that, even in the realm of taboos, from the outset, there is full consciousness of the relation—and a potential conflict—between the objective and the subjective. Any theory denying this is a construct divorced from the evidence. In the case of Uzzah, for instance, David, it is recorded, gets downright angry with the Almighty.[29] (Recognition of the victim's devotion remains even if we follow pious translators or emenders in substituting 'sad' for 'angry'.)

Few motifs are more prominent in ancient tales throughout the world than error and ignorance, and this I would almost call it obsession extends to all walks of life. Greek tradition is so full of, and attaches such weight to, doings and sufferings from misjudgement that Aristotle can identify it as the mainspring of tragedy.[30] The Bible is equally rich in elaborations of the theme: Jacob, disguised as Esau, obtains the blessing due to his elder brother and,

---

[24] See my *Civil Disobedience in Antiquity*, 1972, pp. 75 ff.
[25] Callimachus, *Hymns* 5.70 ff.
[26] Exodus 19.12 f.
[27] I Samuel 6.19; cp. Numbers 4.20.
[28] II Samuel 6.1 ff.
[29] II Samuel 6.8; cp. Leviticus 10.3 ff.
[30] Aristotle, *Poetics* 11.

years later, finds himself married to Leah, disguised as her younger sister Rachel;[31] Uriah unsuspectingly transmits a letter with his death verdict to his general;[32] and so on. Perhaps the primordial Aristotelian tragic hero—*kibheyakhol*—is God, who does not reckon with the serpent frustrating his design.[33] (One could re-write Milton from this angle.) Considering this striking concern with the problem, one wonders how the denial of early insight could have become current among legal historians. In a similar context,[34] I submitted that a doctrine like that here combated manages at the same time to satisfy two deep contradictory needs, notorious for marring research into the past: one, to look down on the 'primitives' from the height of our progress, the other, to look up to them from the depth of our decadence. The former is obviously met by imagining them as not, like us, subtle enough to perceive the state of mind behind the crude act. However, to the latter, too, on closer examination, this theory proves responsive. It makes it possible to picture those people as not, like us, squeamish, sentimental, sicklied over with the pale cast of thought, but hitting back at an aggressor like true men, without bothering about niceties. It is such a comfortable position—I feel like a spoilsport.

2.

The first statutes making allowance for error or ignorance concern acts that count as criminal only because of extraordinary, invisible circumstances of which one might easily be oblivious. The oldest extant provision in point is from Assyria, second half of the second millenium B.C.[35] It exempts from punishment a man who has intercourse with another man's wife, unaware of her status. To sleep with a woman is not, by itself, a crime. It does become one if she is married to somebody else. But this attribute of hers is not manifest. In fact, in a polygamous culture, and especially if no elaborate, public rites are required for marriage and/or divorce, an outsider must quite often be in the dark. Hence the relatively early

---

[31] Genesis 27, 29.16 ff. On this particular mode of retaliation, see my article in *Oxford Journal of Legal Studies*, vol. 1, pp. 53 ff.

[32] II Samuel 11.14 ff.

[33] See my *Civil Disobedience in Antiquity*, 1972, pp. 60 f.

[34] See my *Roman Law*, 1969, p. 172, referring to the widespread view that intention or absence of it made no difference in ancient law because it made no difference in ancient ethics.

[35] Middle Assyrian Laws 14.

heeding of mistake here. Proof is less of an obstacle than usual, in fact, the presumption is almost in favour of the excuse.

An episode from the life of Samson is worth noting.[36] His marriage with a Philistine woman is of the *beenu* type: she resides with her father and he from time to time calls on her. If a husband is fed up with a wife living with him, divorce, however informal, will involve some action on his part: he will tell her to leave, put her out of doors or the like. In a *beenu* union, prior to the requirement of a form, he may simply discontinue his visits. But at what moment can one be sure that it is all over? A long, angry absence of Samson induces his father-in-law to conclude that his daughter is free and he gives her to somebody else. Subjectively, he, she, the new husband and their friends participating in one way or another are all above reproach. None the less when Samson returns, he wreaks terrible vengeance on them. Whether, at the time, in a trial of such a case, mistake could already be pleaded, it is difficult to say. Definitely the complication is understood: the father-in-law does explain why he did what he did and indeed offers Samson another daughter in the place of the re-married one. Samson, however, is happy to have some cause for inflicting harm on the national enemy.

A report about Abraham and the beautiful Sarah at Gerar constitutes an ex professo discussion of the question.[37] He is afraid that if she were known to be his wife, he would be murdered in order that she become available. So he introduces her as his sister, having persuaded her to fall in with this scheme. The king takes her into his harem, whereupon God threatens him with death for appropriating a married woman. But he bravely challenges the justice of this verdict, seeing how he was misled. In the end he is upheld except, of course, that he has to return her. Well, there is a little more. He is in need of Abraham's prayer for him and, further, he makes a considerable payment as homage to Sarah's respectability—a striking instance of the attitude outlined above: even where internal decency excuses, the objective wrong receives a measure of acknowledgment.

At a pre-Biblical stage of the saga, he had intercourse with her. His reprieve by God, despite this fact, was designed to serve as

---

[36] Judges 14 f.
[37] Genesis 20.

guidance to human tribunals, to advocate a regulation like the Assyrian one just cited. The case was well chosen, involving not just a mistake on the part of the accused but a mistake due to deception by the very party—the husband—for whose benefit the harsh treatment of adultery is chiefly intended. The account in Genesis represents God as intervening before intercourse has taken place: it is indeed because of the king's purity of heart that he is prevented from the terrible deed. The author of this version is unwilling to admit that Sarah could actually have been defiled. While his revision renders the tale less directly usable as a legal model, it implies a deep probing into the psychology and theology of mistake.[38] Deliberate concealment of the wife's status, incidentally, is a not uncommon stratagem, serving a variety of ends. In the story before us, the couple are anxious to ensure the husband's safety. But we find it resorted to also in order to entrap a guy, catch him in flagranti and blackmail him: even under a system where subjective righteousness is a good defence, he could not be certain he would be believed, and in any case he might be concerned about his reputation.[39]

In Greece, the Draconian inscription is instructive:[40] you are not liable if you kill a comrade in battle, mistaking him for an enemy. Killing in battle is in order; it is in fact what you are there for. Naturally, however, this licence does not extend to your own side. But, as in the case of a married woman, the distinctive quality invalidating the rule is not immediately obvious—especially if Greek fights Greek—and, in the heat of a melee, investigation is impracticable. (Interestingly, Sophocles's Oedipus argues that you cannot be expected when attacked by an assassin—as he was by Laius—to stop to enquire whether maybe he was your father.[41]) We must bear in mind that uniforms were not then de rigueur: the Gileadites recognized the Ephraimites by their pronunciation of *shibboleth*,[42] and Thucydides, too, mentions dialect as a means of identification in inter-Hellenic strife.[43] Able generals such as Gideon on occasion

---

[38] See above, pp. 51 f., for one facet.
[39] Cp. Demosthenes 49 (Against Neaera) 41.
[40] Demosthenes 23 (Against Aristocrates) 53.
[41] Sophocles, *Oedipus at Colonus* 992 ff. See my article in *California Law Review*, vol. 68, 1980, p. 310.
[42] Judges 12.5 f.
[43] Thucydides 4.3.3, 41.2.

succeeded in so confusing enemy troops that there would be wholesale mutal slaughter among them.[44]

A passage in Sophocles's Antigone concerns mistake of law, not as yet marked off from mistake of fact.[45] Here, too, it is unfamiliarity with a most exceptional, not readily anticipated development that might lead to discharge. The heroine buries her brother who has ended in disgrace, despite a royal ordinance forbidding his burial on pain of death. The king's first question, as she is brought before him, is whether she was acquainted with his edict. Which implies that ignorance would be a valid plea. In general, it is your bounden duty to bury a relative. The ban here is a very special measure and one not concretised in outward, visible signs. It would be rash, without more evidence, to conclude that ignorance of more ordinary laws would in that period avert the sanction.

With these lines from the Antigone we may contrast an incident in Samuel, where missing the announcement of a surprise taboo nearly costs Jonathan his life.[46] His father Saul places a curse on any soldier taking food before a battle with the Philistines is over. He, not having heard of it, eats wild honey which enables him greatly to contribute to the victory. But on a sign of displeasure from heaven, an enquiry is held and his transgression comes to light. Saul sentences him to death; and it is only the protest of the people that saves him. Evidently, moral innocence is here of no avail. It plays no part even in the protest, which is based entirely on the consideration that the man to whom so much is due deserves better. Still, once again, we must beware of too sweeping deductions. The interdict disregarded is not a secular one; it is a curse, thus directly involving the higher powers. As I have remarked already, in this sacred sphere, strict literalism persists much longer. A further point, which I do not, however, propose to elaborate, is that, conceivably, in a earlier form of the narrative, Jonathan contravened the injunction in full knowledge.

At this juncture, it is necessary to cast a glance at a major achievement of the laws of holiness which has had an impact far beyond its original field. We have seen that, where error or ignorance leads to breach of a taboo, it takes quite long for people to

---

[44] Judges 7.22.
[45] Sophocles, *Antigone* 448 f. See my *Civil Disobedience in Antiquity*, 1972, pp. 7 f.
[46] I Samuel 14.24 ff.

be confident that heaven will refrain from or mitigate retribution. Yet perhaps the majority of these regulations are of the kind I have just described, i.e. the wrongful nature of the act is far from conspicuous. You may easily not realize that you are in a state of uncleanness precluding you from entering the sanctuary; or that the food before you is withdrawn from profane use. Jacob, waking up from the famous dream of the ladder, is full of fear because he unwittingly slept on hallowed ground; luckily, the deity accepts his offering.[47] Moses is warned by God in time not to approach the burning bush.[48] It is a dangerous world. No wonder, once levitical legislation does get properly under way, the problem receives a comprehensive solution: if you slip up in this fashion, certain sacrifices and/or payments will put things right. There is technical terminology, a verb *shaghagh* or *shagha*, 'to go astray', and even a noun, *sheghagha*.

What renders this evolution important for the general criminal law is the fact that, in the Book of Numbers,[49] the priests subsume under the heading *sheghagha* various instances of accidental homicide, i.e. homicide not from error or ignorance but, say, where you aim a stone at a bird and it hits a person. A daring feat of synthesis:[50] henceforth, throughout the legal system, the word may denote any absence of evil intent as a basis for relief. The LXX and Vulgate cannot quite keep up with it, having to distinguish between *agnoia* or *ignorantia* in the levitical precepts[51] and *akousios* or *nolens* in connection with homicide. Curiously, the semantic development of German *Versehen* is remotely comparable to that of *sheghagha* —maybe due to Luther's treatment of the term. But it is too complicated a matter here to pursue.

In course of time, penal justice goes beyond the first hesitant steps and attaches relevance to mistake even as to a point less easily mistaken than a woman's status or a soldier's nationality. As often, liberalization of the law is anticipated by religious and ethical teaching which need not grapple to the same extent with practical obstacles like precariousness of evidence or popular resistance. Thus, Aristotle, for example, takes a most progressive stand, ex-

---

[47] Genesis 28.16 ff.
[48] Exodus 3.5.
[49] Numbers 35.9 ff., cp. Joshua 20.1 ff.
[50] For a sophisticated priestly form in this chapter, see below, pp. 100 ff.
[51] E.g. Leviticus 22.14.

onerating virtually any transgression in non-culpable unawareness of essential elements.[52] But law gets there too though, needless to say, always with more reservation.

Jewish law has things worked out pretty fully by Talmudic times.[53] Exactly how far back this position is to be dated I leave open. It so happens that an incident of mistake in the New Testament is the early type, involving an unusual, hidden quality.[54] During an interrogation by the Sanhedrin, Paul, being struck in the face at the order of the high priest, curses the latter. To curse this chief dignitary is a grave offence and the bystanders do not fail to comment on it. However, Paul's declaration that he did not realize who it was immediately ends the affair. Basically, it is the kind of mistake that we found in the ancient provisions about intercourse with somebody else's wife and killing one of your own side in war.

3.

While law, then, finds it hard to deal with mistake in crime, myth, sage, drama and historiography love the subject and never tire of exploring its many departments. The examples adduced above are a tiny fraction of the material. As for the Bible, take the Joseph epic—the father misled about his favourite's disappearance, the latter incarcerated on a trumped-up charge, and a huge hide-and-seek when his brothers visit Egypt.[55] Or the deaths of the Canaanite general Sisera and the Assyrian general Holofernes at the hand of the women charming them into overtrust.[56] Or the several varieties of false prophets.[57] Or the despisers of the gospel, among them, at one time, Paul himself who abetted the stoning of Stephanus.[58] As for Greece, Alcmene entertains Zeus who has donned the shape of her husband; the daughters of Pelias dismember him persuaded that he will come back to life rejuvenated; the mother of Pentheus and her sisters in a Bacchic frenzy fall upon him who appears to them to be a wild beast; Cephalus hurls his spear at Procris mistaking her for a deer; Theseus curses his chaste son Hip-

---

[52] Aristotle, *Nicomachean Ethics* 3.1.17.1111a, 3.5.8 f. 1113b f., 5.8.6 ff. 1135b f.
[53] Mishnah Sanhedrin 9.2, Babylonian Sanhedrin 79a.
[54] Acts 22.30 ff., Exodus 22.27.
[55] Genesis 37 ff.
[56] Judges 5.17 ff., Judith 12.11 ff.
[57] Deuteronomy 13.2 ff., 18.20 ff.
[58] Matthew 13.14 f., John 9.39 f., Luke 23.34, Acts 7.58, 8.1.

polytus whom he thinks guilty of incest; the Thebans succeed in occupying Plataea before the war is official and, in turn, the Plataeans organize resistance unsuspected by the conquerors.[59] Germanic romances also come to mind: Hildebrand and Hadubrand who, not knowing that they are father and son, fight one another, Siegfried who, having been given a magic potion to make him forget about Brunhild, weds Kriemhild. One could go on and on.

To be sure, quite a few of these episodes are connected—more or less closely—with legal developments. But concern with the disarray caused by error and ignorance clearly goes far beyond the problem of its treatment in court: it extends to all major doings in life. Significantly, whereas killing under a misapprehension is a favourite theme of story-tellers, accidental killing, despite its great legal interest, does not attract them at all. The entire Biblical corpus records one accidental homicide, and even here this aspect receives no special attention: one of the two prostitutes who bring their dispute before King Solomon has overlain her baby.[60]

Such enormous, one-sided preoccupation must stem from a profound level of the psyche. The point is that these flaws of the mind horrify since they interfere where we can least brook interference, where we most wish to be unhampered: at the very centre of planned action. When things go wrong owing to outer forces, when accident or the like brings about an unwanted result, that is something ordinary, befalling every rank of existence, nature, beast, man. A lightning, a disease, a drought, a sudden collision—deplorable as these evils may be, there is nothing in the world not exposed to them. But when things turn out wrong because we proceed from fallacious premises, when the result that we did want reveals itself as inimical, that is a blow to our distinctively human make-up, that hits us where the hurt to our effort, hope and pride is cruellest, that reveals our fallibility as thinking beings intent on controlling our affairs, lifting them above the ordinary plane.

Aristotle sees the essence of the tragic in the downfall of one favoured by fortune and apparently its master through a miscalculation which indeed he realizes—but too late.[61] This focus on the discovery of an error has been found strange, so strange as to

---

[59] Thucydides 2.2.3 ff.; see C. Schneider, *Information und Absicht bei Thukydides*, 1974, pp. 77 ff.
[60] I Kings 3.16 ff.
[61] *Poetics* 10 f.

be declared a hangover from a phase before the writing of tragedy: its real application was to the ritual of Dionysus, which resembled that of Osiris, which in turn involved the discovery of the slain god's corpse by his wife.[62] Whether or not there is anything in this genealogy may be left undecided. It is certainly not needed: the view set forth in the Art of Poetry reflects an attitude powerfully present in the sources, Eastern and Western, from the earliest times. Indeed, something like it may have been formulated in the preceding century. Thucydides, it has recently been shown,[63] in his Peloponnesian War, gives its full dramatic force to the moment when you become aware of an illusion; and the verb *lanthano*, 'to escape notice', occurs more than fifty times.

A prominent figure in medical research, L. Thomas, contends[64] that growing comprehension, by means of science in particular, distinguishes us from the rest of nature. As we are only at the beginning of this process, science is ever uncertain, 'shifting ... revising ... then heaving itself explosively apart to redesign everything'. This changeability is of the very essence of our enterprise, 'a celebration of human fallibility'.

He makes a strong case. But the point here of interest is that, palpably, he is no less anxious about our proneness to straying than those thinkers of bygone times. And, in a later part of his article, the tragic prevails over the triumphant: 'Such things as happen to human nations, error piled on error, could never happen in a school of fish. It is, when you think about it, a humiliation'. Aristotle *redivivus*.

4.

So far I have taken error and ignorance in the sense to which we are accustomed from criminal jurisprudence: misinformation or lack of information as to a relevant fact or law. You charge a borrower interest because you erroneously think him a gentile or because you are ignorant of the illegality of interest among Jews. I shall now add some remarks on a less pedestrian variety: error and ignorance in the sense of a flaw in or absence of deeper under-

---

[62] See G. Murray, in *Aristotle, On the Art of Poetry*, trsl. by I. Baywater, *Preface*, p. 14.
[63] See C. Schneider, *op. cit.*, pp. 81, 85.
[64] *Harvard Magazine*, vol. 83 no. 1, Sept.-Oct. 1980, pp. 19 ff.

standing, as when we say of a gang of murderers or burglars 'they do not know any better'. The serpent encouraging our ancestors to get 'to know good and evil' and the Delphic admonition 'know thyself' envisage, not an amassing of material, but a grasp of our standing in the universe, our nature, our authentic destiny—a quite different range of consciousness.

Paradoxically, while inadequacy of relevant information rules out or at least reduces moral guilt, inadequacy of understanding in general counts as its very hallmark. When Hosea exclaims,[65] 'My people are destroyed for being without knowledge', he means 'without discernment of God's will'; and he is referring, not to your taking somebody else's purse in the belief it is yours, but to dishonesty, whoring, bloodshed. The Cyclops Polyphemus is 'savage, knowing neither usages nor dooms'.[66] For Clytemnaestra's father, her son and executioner Orestes is 'void of insight'—a miscreant.[67] The Fourth evangelist plays upon the two levels I am distinguishing:[68] 'For judgment I am come', Jesus proclaims, 'that they who see not—i.e. the uninformed ones—might see—i.e. understand—and that they who see—i.e. the informed ones—might be made blind—in the deeper sense. And the Pharisees said, Are we blind also—i.e. do we, with all our learning, not understand? Jesus said, If you were blind—i.e. uninformed—you would have no sin, but now you say, We see—i.e. you boast of information and understanding—therefore your sin remains'. Here, too, failure to understand is the real enormity.

The line between the two kinds of shortcoming is admittedly fuzzy. Polyphemus, or Kipling's 'lesser breeds without the law', in most contexts appear to suffer mostly from defective understanding, but in some rather from defective information. A wavering between these approaches underlies much of Talmudic and New Testament thought about pagans. It is also, of course, possible to be definitely devoid of both information and understanding—as witness anyone critical of my propositions.

In Greece, with a premium on carrying an idea to its logical conclusion, from around 500 B.C. it is noticed that one could look on an ordinary parricide whose aim is to come into his father's wealth

---

[65] Hosea 4.6.
[66] Homer, *Odyssey* 9.215.
[67] Euripides, *Orestes* 493.
[68] John 9.39 f.

as acting by mistake, along with Oedipus. 'Nobody is wittingly evil', we hear from Epicharmos.[69] Socrates and Plato take it up in earnest, declaring old-fashioned retribution pointless. A criminal would not have done what he did had he been alive to the adverse consequences for his well-being either in daily life or spiritual.[70] (The Delphic 'knowing oneself' repeatedly appears in this context.[71]) Hence the proper response is instruction. To reinforce it, and also to teach bystanders, the infliction of some hurt on him may indeed be called for; but it is not punishment of a moral wrong—being mistaken, he did not commit any. What if he persists transgressing? Then he suffers from an incurable disease, eating up both himself and the community, and he had better be put out of the way.[72]

Instruction, deterrence, treatment are all three employed long before this period to suppress antisocial behaviour. (In my last lecture, I shall present Pentateuchic statutes concerning sexual offences and homicide modelled on medical prescriptions.[73]) Alas, these methods are hardly less open to abuse than the more spontaneous ones like vengeance or righting the balance. Arguably, the Socratic-Platonic scheme itself illustrates this by its proposal of death or banishment for one who just does not learn. The press in this country keeps voicing its misgivings about regimes that subject dissidents to psychiatric care; and while I am readying my typescript for publication, the fifty-two Americans released from Iran are being flown to a military hospital in West-Germany so that any who under the stress of imprisonment might have taken to their captors could be nursed to recovery.[74]

However, there is no doubt as to the high-mindedness of the philosophical approach and as to its seriousness in trying to deal with the total personality rather than a disjointed segment—though the hardnosed bulk of Athenians must have been all the more upset. To them, the turning of a scoundrelly disposition, hitherto obvious-

---

[69] H. Diels, *Die Fragmente der Vorsokratiker*, 6th ed., ed. W. Kranz, 1951, p. 199.
[70] Expanded, touchingly, by Epictetus, *Discourses* reported by Arrian 4.1.114 ff.
[71] Plato, *Protagoras* 343B, Xenophon, *Memorabilia* 4.2.24.
[72] Plato, *Lesser Hippias* 376, *Protagoras* 324 ff., 343, 345 ff., *Apology* 25 f., *Gorgias* 460 f., 478 ff., 525 ff., *Republic* 380, *Timaeus* 86 ff., *Laws* 731, 854, 860 f., 934, Xenophon, *Memorabilia* 4.2.24.
[73] See below, pp. 100ff.
[74] My friend Jim Mosher suggests that I might add a reference to Garry Trudeau's Doonesbury cartoon in *San Francisco Chronicle*, 30 January 1981, p. 64.

ly damnable, into an alibi, proof of error or ignorance precluding punishment, must have seemed, as regards mode of reasoning, a typically sophistic extension of the genuine cases in the field—such as the Draconian mix-up in battle—and as regards effect, a pernicious undermining of the sense of responsibility: why practise self-restraint if you may plead not guilty to any outrage?

There is a great deal in these objections. The latter comes up time and again in the annals of penology, whenever a theory smacking of the Socratic-Platonic one is advanced. Thus, psychoanalysis is widely perceived as insinuating that *tout comprendre c'est tout pardonner*: its focus on a fatal, covert mechanism behind the outbreak appears to leave no room for blame. (To be sure, as it also lays bare your horrid motives when you are wishing your sister a happy birthday, one might just as well get the message that *tout comprendre c'est tout condamner*.) Many law-and-order persons are deeply suspicious of this movement and both Stalin and Hitler proscribed it. To go by a newspaper report,[75] Pope John Paul II recently reminded a group of visitors that in the view of the church man is not left entrapped, not continually at the mercy of lust 'as the Freudian libido would have it'. To return to Socrates, to this day, the ferociousness of his opponents continues to puzzle: 'it would seem almost incredible', writes a translator in the Loeb series,[76] 'that the Athenian court voted for condemnation, if we did not know the fact'. Perhaps too little thought has been given to what the *bienpensants* must have felt about his apparent decriminalization of crime. My hunch is that it was a major cause of his undoing: such preaching had to be stopped.

Plato, in The Apology, depicts him as following an approved rhetorical scheme of defence:[77] your best line is to disclaim the deed, your next-best to prefer some such explanation as that it was justified, an accident, due to a mistake. Socrates denies having corrupted the youth: line one. Moreover—line two, of interest for this discussion[78]—should he be held to have done so, he must have acted inadvertently, without knowledge of the injurious nature of his advice: who would wittingly lead astray those around him, thereby making it likely that he himself will suffer harm through

---

[75] See *San Francisco Examiner*, October 30, 1980, p. A3.
[76] See H. N. Fowler, *Plato*, vol. 1, *Loeb Classical Library*, 1943, p. 66.
[77] See my article in *California Law Review*, vol. 68, 1980, pp. 302 ff.
[78] Plato, *Apology* 13.25C ff.

their wickedness? So if he did corrupt the youth, he ought to be, not arraigned, but offered lessons.

Evidently, the knowledge here contemplated is not a single, simple piece of information. To be clear as to what does or does not constitute corruption of the youth, you need to have cracked the most perplexing riddles of existence. He is demanding, then, the same consideration for non-possession of this, we might say Delphic, wisdom that was by then accorded to non-possession of certain specific data. Note that his argument practically rules out any prosecution of the wrong in question: either it has not been committed or, if it has, mistake renders it immune. True, for this particular offence, the converse also holds: corruption of the youth is so malleable a concept, so dependent on the definer's opinion, that any teacher not toeing the line might find himself in the dock. But this aspect, needless to say, will not irk the powers-that-be, whereas that brought up by Socrates will very much indeed.

Two more comments on his oration. First, so long as you have a modicum of intelligence, he asserts, you will never wittingly demoralize your entourage, if only because you foresee that ultimately you yourself may be a victim of their depravity. Plausible enough up to a point. Besides, it is surely directed against The Clouds by Aristophanes. Some traits there ascribed to Socrates are repudiated in so many words in The Apology.[79] In the passage under notice, the play is not named, but the public of the time can scarcely have missed the allusion. For it is just this kind of tit-for-tat that befalls the speaker and a disciple of his in the comedy.[80] A father, having been trained by him in sophistry, sends him his son too, hoping he will learn the same tricks and help him dupe his creditors. However, the son, returned, uses his quibbles to justify beating up his parents. In the end, the father sets fire to Socrates's school, all the while mimicking the master's mannerisms. In The Apology, Socrates counters that nobody in their senses, and certainly not himself, would proceed like those caricatures of educators.

Second, his official indictment was for *aseby*, impiety. The earliest instance prserved in the sources is the trial of Aeschylus, some sixty years before. He, presumably in a drama, divulged a mystery of the

---

[79] Plato, *Apology* 3.19A ff.
[80] The variety of talion involved is the same as in the Jacob narrative quoted above, pp. 55 f.

goddess Demeter. He was acquitted—on the ground of ignorance: he had not known that the matter was a secret. It was, of course, a famous affair; famous enough to be adverted to by Aristotle, quite shorthand since he could rely on the details being familiar, as illustrating one of the six types of ignorance—namely, ignorance of precisely what you are doing.[81] What is worth observing here is that, in contrast to Socrates's plea, this one referred to sheer lack of information. It is comparable to, say, the excuse Creon would have accepted from Antigone—that she had not heard of his edict forbidding her brother's burial—or, in the Bible, Jacob's unawareness that he was lying down to sleep on a sacred site. I wonder whether, when Socrates or Plato contended that the charge of impiety must fail because of lack of understanding, he was stimulated by the illustrious precedent, conscious of radically expanding its scope.

We may now ask: is there an analogous Jewish strand where the sinner's blindness, instead of being a reproach, exonerates? There is, though, as we shall see, with a tremendous proviso. Two quotes from the Old Testament. In Isaiah,[82] the Suffering Servant is the comfort of those who 'like sheep have gone astray'—obviously not soldiers who have killed the wrong guy in a melee but proper villains: their moral helplessness is emphasized in mitigation. And that marvellously universalist Book of Jonah ends with a pardon for Nineveh 'wherein are more than sixscore persons who do not know their right hand and their left hand, and also much cattle': vengeance is stayed in deference to lack of understanding. This text is of extraordinary importance for the history of sin, punishment and forgiveness in Judaism. To outsiders, it might seem tucked away in a recondite part of Scripture. In reality, Jonah has been a prescribed Lesson from the Prophets on the Day of Atonement, hence continuously influential, for some two thousand years.[83] Again, as for the Talmud, Eliezer the Great of the first century A.D. finds a verse in Numbers on which to base the teaching that even the deliberate, presumptuous transgressions of the community are treated by God as committed in error.[84] Lastly, as a New Testament example, we may think of 'Father, forgive them, for they

---

[81] Aristotle, *Nicomachean Ethics* 3.1.17.111a; see my *Civil Disobedience in Antiquity*, 1972, pp. 72, 116 f.
[82] Isaiah 53.6.
[83] Babylonian Megillah 31a.
[84] Siphre on Numbers 15.25.

know not what they do'.[85] Very possibly, the famous words, missing from several early manuscripts, were uttered by Stephanus as he was stoned[86] and then transferred to Jesus. At any rate, the innocent victim magnanimously prays for those who, though given all essential information, are slaying him: their want of true comprehension makes them deserving of pity rather than judgment. I refrain from drawing on the Rabbinic and early Christian discussion of heathendom and its vices: there are many texts in point[87] but they are subtle and complicated and I must not detain you too long.

Yet there is this difference from Socratic philosophy, that in Jewish and Jewish-Christian documents lack of understanding spells not guilty or less guilty only vis-à-vis heaven. Not once is it invoked, like lack of a critical datum, to invalidate an accusation under human law or ethics. Our creaturely weakness, our akinness to sheep (Isaiah) and cattle (Jonah), our failure to recognize good and evil, will, it is hoped, exculpate us in the eyes of a merciful deity. It may even be paid a measure of attention, slighter or greater according to the offender's circumstances, by a this-wordly tribunal. But it does not, on earth, basically rid a misdeed of its moral imputability, still less does it warrant a general denial of inner, moral viciousness. A profound, religious sense of being at sea, that is, never conduces to a sophistic questioning of state justice. In this life, however flawed our intellect and emotions, we are responsible for our conduct towards our fellow-beings.

---

[85] Luke 23.34.
[86] Hegesippus, *Ecclesiastical History* 2.23.16.
[87] E.g. Rabbi Tarphon's distinction between heathen and heretic in Tosephta Shabbath 13.5.

EXCURSUS TO LECTURE II

After the lecture, an alumnus of the University of Judaism told me of the Head of a Yeshivah passing by the dormitory on a Sabbath and seeing through the window three students smoking. He summons them to appear before him. The first says, 'I forgot that it was the Sabbath'; the second, 'I forgot that you must not smoke on a Sabbath'; and the third, 'I forgot to draw the curtains'.

Well, two thousand years ago, No. 1 and No. 2, having transgressed by mistake of fact and law respectively, would have had to bring a sin-offering. With this distinction, that No. 1, if the following week he again forgot about Sabbath, he would be committing a second mistake of fact and a second transgression, hence be liable to a second sin-offering; whereas No. 2, if the following week he was still forgetful of the smoking prohibition, he would be continuing in the same mistake of law and the same transgression, hence could get away with one sin-offering.[1] No. 3's sin is deliberate, punishment to be meted out by God. Yet, possibly, even he has a mitigating circumstance in his favour. He had intended to remain unnoticed—no doubt chiefly in order to avert exposure but, maybe, also in order to avoid scandal, flouting religion, ḥillul hashshem.[2] Does this not constitute hypocrisy?, I hear today's enlightened youth ask. The answer is: yes, more or less according to the situation. A more basic objection might be that two thousand years ago they did not smoke.

---

[1] Mishnah Shabbath 7.1.
[2] Babylonian Moed Qatan 17a, Qiddushin 40a; see my article in *Theology*, vol. 72, 1969, p. 294.

LECTURE III

THE FORM IS THE MESSAGE

The form of a statement usually reveals a good deal, apart from its content.[1] Of course, it is never possible to appreciate either in strict isolation from the other. However, exclusive interest in material is so common as to justify a call to restore the balance. The fact is that the slightest nuance in style is likely to signify something. A report that 'Carter is coming to San Francisco' is not the same as 'the President is coming to San Francisco'. In the field of legislation, we shall presently see, 'If a man steals a sheep, he shall be hanged' is not the same as 'Whoever steals a sheep shall be hanged', though at first blush one might think so.

Before going *in medias res*, a reservation: a structure once established is apt to be carried on mechanically, in which case it may tell us more about the past than the present. Take the way mail is addressed. In Germany, where I grew up, I was taught to put first the addressee's name, Hermann Müller, then the place, Ulm, then the street, Kaiserstrasse, and lastly the house number, 12. This order becomes intelligible when we consider that, at one time, mostly, name and place were all that was needed: Hermann Müller, Ulm. Later it became necessary to add the street, yet later the house number. Today the arrangement makes little sense and they are about to adopt the British-American one with its clear progress from particular to general: name, house number, street, place. It is questionable, however, whether even here logic was a factor at the outset. Formerly, a person's dwelling was often more or less part of the name—John Smith the Mill, Peter Low the Oakwood—and it may well have been in this role that house number and street obtained their position before the place on an English address. Arguably, a rational modern address constructed *de novo* would begin with the place, there would follow street and house number, and the name would come at the end.

In law and related areas, where tradition is strong, a good many modalities outlive their meaning.[2] The 'whereas' introduction of a

---

[1] See Excursus 1, below, pp. 117 ff.
[2] See D. Mellinkoff, *The Language of the Law*, 1963, pp. 290 ff.

statute has a history taking us back to the Greek philosophers' debate as to whether a legislator should set forth his reasons.[3] Yet it became so time-worn that often we are told scarcely more than: 'Whereas it is expedient to lay down the following provisions'.[4] Or think of the piling up of synonyms—'this object shall not be damaged, injured, hurt, harmed, broken, split, scratched'. In a period of hairsplittingly rigid interpretation, it might be a safeguard,[5] but it continued—or should I say, continues?—long after that. (It does remain useful to the lawyer whose client believes such lingo needed and pays for it.)

Still, a vestige at least of the original import normally lingers on. Let us look at the pair 'If a man steals a sheep, he shall hanged' and 'Whoever, or he who, steals a sheep shall be hanged'. I have discussed it before[6] but present it again because it is such a straightforward—if somewhat boring—illustration, or test, of my theme. A court will certainly come to the same decision no matter which alternative it has before it. The substance, then, is identical—at any rate, for most practical purposes. Yet even here it pays to take notice of the patterns. They turn out to derive from quite distinct evolutionary stages and, furthermore, to carry a little of their primary equipment with them to this day.

The conditional clause goes back to a much older mode of lawmaking than the relative. It tells the occurrence to be regulated, 'a man steals a sheep', and all it does to raise it from a story to a model is to put 'if' in front. Actually, in Nordic compilations, we find a phrasing even nearer the bare narrative, with no 'if' but merely a 'now': 'Now a slave runs away',[7] 'Now a man becomes a slayer',[8] 'Now a slayer swims out to a boat'.[9] And there is the transitional 'now if': 'Now if men fall in battle'.[10] By contrast, the relative clause, 'whoever steals' or 'he who steals', instead of

---

[3] Plato, *Laws* 4.718 ff.

[4] *Probate of First Offender Act*, 1887, J. M. Lely, *The Statutes of Practical Utility*, vol. 3, 1894, p. 164; *India Church Act*, 1927, *The Statutes printed by authority*, 3rd rev. ed., vol. 19, 1950, p. 355.

[5] See my discussion in *Buffalo Law Review*, vol. 20, 1970, pp. 41 ff.

[6] See above, Preface, p. X.

[7] *Norwegisches Recht*, Gulathing, translated into German by R. Meissner, 1935, p. 57.

[8] *Landrecht des Königs Magnus Hakonarson*, edited and translated into German by R. Meissner, 1941, pp. 102 f.

[9] *Norwegisches Recht*, p. 107.

[10] *Landrecht*, p. 179.

reciting an occurrence, introduces a person defined by his action: the story is replaced by a category. The step will be best comprehended by thinking of the question to which each of the two forms makes answer. The conditional presupposes the question: 'What shall be done if so-and-so happens?'—surely about the earliest enquiry directed to a lawgiver. Answer: 'If so-and-so happens, if a man steals a sheep, he shall be hanged'. The relative presupposes a question that has advanced far beyond the emergency 'if so-and-so happens', being at home with abstraction, thinking in terms of classes: 'What shall be done to such-and-such a class, to whoever steals a sheep?' Answer: 'Whoever steals a sheep shall be hanged'.

No wonder Hammurabi, the Twelve Tables, the genuine Mispatim in Exodus,[11] are dominated by 'if', while in Neo-Babylonian laws, laws around the time of Augustus, laws in Leviticus,[12] 'whoever' is no less frequent. We have to do with a universal phenomenon: it takes a long period of occurrence-orientation to be able to reach category-orientation, and some legal cultures do not get there at all, remain what we might call folk-law. I should add that since I first dealt with this matter, Reuven Yaron has drawn attention to the relative in proclamations like 'Whoever is fearful, let him return',[13] 'What man that will begin to fight Ammon, he shall be head'.[14] This usage may well have played a major part in the development.[15]

The generalizing, systematizing thrust of the breakthrough from 'if' to 'whoever' or 'he who' comes out beautifully in King Alfred's code. In the midst of a chapter with one 'if' after another, there is this provision: 'If anyone seeks the King's life, he shall lose his life and all his possessions'. Then follows the one exception: 'So we ordain for all estates, too, commoners as well as nobles—he who seeks his master's life shall lose his life and all his possessions'.[16] The 'he who' part is clearly marked as an innovation. Emphatically, dramatically, generously (generously to the ins, that is) it extends punishability from one plotting against the King—very narrow—to

---

[11] Exodus 21 ff.
[12] Leviticus 20.
[13] Judges 7.3.
[14] Judges 10.18.
[15] See R. Yaron, *The Laws of Eshnunna*, 1969, pp. 67 f.
[16] *Die Gesetze der Angelsachsen*, edited and translated into German by F. Liebermann, 1903, vol. 1, pp. 50 f.

one plotting against his superior—all-inclusive. It is here that 'he who' makes its appearance.

Once a civilisation has adopted the relative, the legislator can choose between it and the conditional; and closer examination reveals that the intrinsic, primary difference never completely ceases to matter. For example, where a law is subdivided into main case and more special case, often the former begins with 'whoever' and the latter with 'if', while the converse is extremely rare. There are scores of Roman statutes, senatusconsults and edicts like this one: 'Through whose-ever wickedness a tomb is interfered with (basic offence) against him I shall give an action for 100,000 sesterces. If anyone makes his habitation in a tomb (aggravated offence), against him I shall give an action for 200,000'.[17] Just so, a U.S. statute runs: 'Whoever wilfully sets fire to any building shall be imprisoned not more than five years. If the building be a dwelling, he shall be imprisoned not more than twenty years'.[18] It is most unlikely that the drafters have reflected on the respective values of 'if' and 'whoever'. They instinctively go on observing them, they just feel that this sounds right and the opposite would sound wrong—which makes the evidence all the more impressive.

I now proceed to three patterns which, I suppose, count as characteristic respectively of Old Testament, New Testament and Tannaitic precepts: 'you shall' or 'you shall not', 'you have heard but I say', 'one does' or 'one does not'. 'You shall' or 'you shall not' is far from widespread. More specifically, it is met neither in the New Testament nor in the Talmud, except, of course, in quotations. The most perfect application is offered by the Ten Commandments: 'Thou shalt not make an image, bow down to them, serve them, take the name of the Lord in vain, do any work on the Sabbath, murder, commit adultery, steal, bear false witness, covet'. We may include a slight variation: 'There shall not be unto thee other gods'.[19] It will be noticed that, throughout, the singular, 'thou', is used, as is the negative 'shalt not'. Hardly accidental: I take it that the singular version of the form preceded the plural one, and, alas, prohibition preceded positive rule.

---

[17] O. Lenel, *Das Edictum Perpetuum*, 3rd ed., 1927, p. 228.
[18] Title 18 of United States Code, *Crimes and Criminal Procedure*, Part I, Crimes, Chapter 5, Arson, Section 81.
[19] Exodus 20.2 ff., Deuteronomy 5.6 ff.

What is the initial background? Let us begin by observing that the directives purport to emanate from highest, absolute authority. Actually, the translation 'thou shalt not' is not quite adequate. In Hebrew, this is indistinguishable from the future, 'thou wilt not'. (The expert will have no difficulty in substituting the correct terminology of Semitic grammar.[20]) The Septuagint, the New Testament quotations and the Vulgate do put the future, *ou phoneuseis, non occides*. We ought to acknowledge an element going beyond what should not be done, on to what will not be done, in other words, a prophetic-predicting-compelling admixture, a spell. Hence a transgressor would be breaking down a sacred barrier, would be placing himself outside the God-determined order of things. When a father sternly admonishes his children 'You will never dishonour the family name', the implications are not dissimilar. (Poor Kelsen. Ought and is are not, then, forever apart. Christian Morgenstern's Korf knew it: *Weil, so schliesst er messerscharf, nicht sein kann was nicht sein darf.*)

We come across here a feature to which I shall return when analysing Tannaitic diction:[21] laws apparently without sanction may yet contain one. The injunctions under review never provide for human enforcement and only now and then add a reminder of heaven's vigilance—for example, 'the Lord will not hold him guiltless that takes his name in vain'. But even in the absence of any such clause, my point is that, originally, 'thou shalt not' as such carries a threat. So long as it has its full force, comprising 'thou wilt not', the consequences of a violation are tremendous—a fall into the abyss.

Next, for the addressee. It is the individual; the male individual, to be precise, as may be gathered from 'thou shalt not covet thy neighbour's wife'. He is spoken to, put under restraint, in the most immediate and gripping fashion, far more immediate than would be 'nobody shall do so and so' or 'this or that shall not be done', far more gripping than the paternal caveats of Wisdom which, typically, are without that domineering 'thou wilt not' touch. It is up to him to comply with these interdicts: they are supported, as just mentioned, by no this-worldly measures in the event of disobedience.

---

[20] Cp. below, pp. 95f.
[21] See below, pp. 85f.

As to substance, it will suffice to notice the concentration on taboos indispensable to the cohesion of a peculiar, religious community. No casuistry: 'Thou shalt not murder'—and not a word as to exactly what the crime consists in or what killings are still permissible or excusable. At the same time, the range covered by the brief list is extraordinarily wide: from false worship to theft, from a gross disruption of peace like adultery to the mere inclination of coveting.

It is with regard to 'Thou shalt not covet' that insensitivity to pattern has fostered a major fallacy. We often hear[22] that an early legislator would not be concerned about an inner lapse. Accordingly, it is concluded, either the Ten Commandments, or at least their final exhortations, are late or the verb traditionally rendered as 'to covet' in reality signifies a concrete act, say, 'to meddle with' or 'to start to meddle with'.

This reasoning is mistaken. Certainly, there are subtle attitudes primitive tribunals are unable to go into. Negligence is one of them. It would be impracticable in 1200 B.C. Palestine to expect a verdict to turn on its presence or absence in the person arraigned. As for coveting, it never anywhere becomes punishable by the secular arm. A statute 'If a man covets another's ox, he shall be fined half his value' would be as utopian today as then. But this does not mean that negligence and coveting are not from time immemorial recognized for what they are and frowned on. No Hebrew, Greek or any other law imposes a penalty on wrath or greed; yet Cain is reproved for the former[23] and Plato asserts that war is caused by the latter.[24] And, while 'If a man covets, he shall be fined' would not make sense at any time, in a God-fearing epoch, however remote, 'Thou shalt not covet' does. This warning 'thou shalt not', which we found to be a communication to the individual of the divine will, with no dependence on any intermediary aid, is highly suitable for inculcating the sinfulness not only of deeds but also of states of mind. The recipient hears: that is what matters. Again, over these prohibitions, we have seen, the Almighty alone stands guard. He, even in the stone age, unlike earthly officers, has no difficulty in

---

[22] See my *Roman Law*, 1969, pp. 163 f.; also the literature quoted by B. Jackson, *Hebrew Union College Annual*, vol. 42, 1971, pp. 197 ff. He does not share the erroneous approach. Nor (as W. D. Davies, who looked through my typescript, reminds me) did C. H. Dodd: see his *Paul to the Romans*, 1932, pp. 108 ff.

[23] Genesis 4.6.

[24] *Phaedo* 66C ff., *Republic* 2.373 D.

unveiling the hidden and determining and carrying out the fitting response.

There is ample corroboration. Just as the deity can deal with internal evil irrespective of external data, so it can with internal good. The King of Gerar, having taken Sarah into his harem under the impression that she is Abraham's sister only, not his wife, successfully reminds God: 'In the simplicity of my heart have I done this'.[25] Parallels abound.

So we may now ask: what setting would produce just this style—a ban from on high, direct to the conscience,[26] devoid of casuistic addenda and capable of reaching into areas beyond terrestrial power? The answer emerges from those ancient Oriental documents which focus on the kind of wrong 'thou shalt not' is primarily meant for. Two quotations. In the Egyptian Book of the Dead, the soul brought before the underworld arbiters affirms: 'I have not killed, I have not instigated any killing, I have not defiled myself, I have not stolen, I have not been covetous, I have not told lies'. In Babylonia, in serious illness, the gods are asked: 'Has he despised father or mother? Has he given petty things and refused important ones? Has he approached the wife of his fellow? Has he shed the blood of his fellow? Has he been sincere with his mouth and false with his heart?'[27]

Here, in final protestation, confession and search into one's past, the scope is precisely that of 'thou shalt not', grave lapses inner as well as outer. In death and mortal sickness everyone, high or low, is utterly alone, exposed, forced to account, without helpers and subterfuges, for what he was really up to—all facade being gone. (The medieval Dies Irae, figuring in Goethe's Faust, contains the lines: *Quidquid latet apparebit*, 'All secrets will be revealed', and *Quem patronum rogaturus*, 'You will have no protector'.) It is, I suggest, this ultimate, desperate situation which, at the outset, the form we are considering envisages. Its essential function is to announce the one route of escape from eternal damnation; or in the imagery of the Book of the Dead, to keep you from being swallowed up by the crocodile instead of stepping into unending bliss. If you stay within the boundaries drawn, and only then, you can face the last

---

[25] Genesis 20.5. See above, pp. 51f., 57f.
[26] See Excursus 2, below, pp. 123ff.
[27] See A. Jirku, *Altorientalischer Kommentar Zum Alten Testament*, 1923, pp. 87 f.

jury—one not to be deceived and weighing up your schemes as well as your execution. (My friend Louis Brown of U.S.C. should be pleased: 'thou shalt not' may be dubbed the earliest specimen of preventive law, designed to avert the calamitous results of sin.) Hence, at the initial stage, the preoccupation with fundamentals, the omission of ifs and buts, the inclusion of internal depravity. Hence another, very different thing. I am struck again by the tenacity with which the original aura of a phrase clings long after the circumstances of its birth are largely forgotten. To this day, the term 'plebiscite' or 'plebiscitarian' has a revolutionary ring, a remnant of the struggle of plebeians against patricians.[28] Similarly, 'thou shalt not' is still strangely powerful: a quality coming down from that ancient setting, the naked soul's choice between ruin and salvation.

To go on to 'one does' or 'one does not'. 'One does': 'When the month of Ab comes in, one reduces joy';[29] 'He who buys fruits from an Uninstructed separates first tithe and second tithe';[30] 'If a buyer of fruits finds among them coins in a bundle, he proclaims them'.[31] 'One does not': 'One does not sell pagans bears or lions or anything dangerous';[32] 'He who undertakes to be an Associate does not sell an Uninstructed wet or dry produce and does not receive him if he wears his ordinary garment (presumed to be unclean)';[33] 'One does not divide a courtyard unless each co-owner will be left with four cubits'.[34] 'One does' and 'one does not' side by side: 'On Purim, women sing dirges for the dead but do not wail';[35] 'One does not let children fast on the Day of Atonement but one trains them a year or two before they come of age';[36] 'The proselyte brings the first-fruits but does not recite the traditional declaration';[37] 'If a man throws a stone in his yard and kills somebody entitled to be there, he goes into exile, if somebody not entitled, he does not go into exile'.[38]

---

[28] See my article in *Tijdschrift voor Rechtsgeschiedenis*, vol. 47, 1979, p. 240.
[29] Mishnah Taanith 4.6.
[30] Babylonian Sotah 48a.
[31] Mishnah Baba Metzia 2.4.
[32] Mishnah Abodah Zarah 1.7.
[33] Mishnah Demai 2.3.
[34] Mishnah Baba Bathra 1.6.
[35] Mishnah Moed Qatan 3.9.
[36] Mishnah Yoma 8.4.
[37] Mishnah Bikkurim 1.4, Deuteronomy 23.3 ff.
[38] Mishnah Makkoth 2.2.

This pattern springs up in the intertestamental era and, by New Testament times, it predominates.

What we have before us is a rule expressed as a fact (once again, a fusion of is and ought). Instead of 'In the month of Ab, one should reduce joy', we are told, 'In the month of Ab, one reduces joy'. This twist occurs in many languages, English among them. An old-order parent may reprove a weeping young son: 'A boy does not cry'. Well, he clearly does, so this is not intended as a portrayal of the situation. It stands for: 'A boy ought not to cry'.

Roughly, the usage no doubt evolves in these stages. The starting-point is a present occurrence: 'They work this morning and do not drink'. Next comes a habitual occurrence: 'Some people work, others drink'. Then a habitual occurrence approved of: 'Decent people work and do not drink', 'Doctors care for their patients'. And finally, the added implication that you should fall in with it. In a speech by the boss to his men or in a class on medical ethics, an observation like 'Decent people work', 'Doctors care', readily gains a normative sense. It is this last step which is relevant to my inquiry. Precisely what is its typical milieu, its specific point?

In English, the part of the verb prominent in this structure is the indicative present. The Oxford Dictionary's definition of 'indicative' is 'stating a thing as a fact'.[39] The nearest Hebrew equivalent is the participle, employed in all the above illustrations. The very first paragraph of the Mishnah opens:[40] 'From when are they reciting the Shema in the evening?'. A more idiomatic rendering will be: 'From when does one recite?'. And its import is: 'From when may one recite?'. That the participle has directive force is confirmed by its alternating with modes of the verb more commonly and openly constraining. Here is a provision about school on late Friday afternoon, when it is important not to miss the beginning of the Sabbath: 'A master is watching how the children read but he himself should not read'.[41] 'Is watching' means 'may watch'; and the second half, 'should not read', does bring in the imperfect. Similar switches are met in the Manual of Discipline of the Dead Sea Essenes: 'The priests shall be (imperfect) blessing and all that enter are saying (participle, evidently as good as the imperfect),

---

[39] H. W. Fowler and F. G. Fowler, *The Concise Oxford Dictionary*, new ed., rev. H. W. Fowler, 1929, p. 580.
[40] Mishnah Berakoth 1.1.
[41] Mishnah Shabbath 1.3.

Amen. And the priests shall continue (perfect with consecutive waw) and all that enter shall open (imperfect) and say (perfect with consecutive waw), Amen'.[42] The same goes for the codes of the primitive Christian community the phrasing of which, we shall soon see, can be inferred from Paul's and Peter's Epistles.

The style plainly covers the religious and the secular, the month of Ab and coins found in a purchase. Since, essentially, the data underlying those precepts are customs—positive, 'one does', or negative, 'one does not'—the variety of normative shades is considerable. We may have to deduce a strict duty, a must or a must not: 'If a man kills somebody entitled to be there, he goes into exile', 'must go'; 'One does not sell pagans anything dangerous', 'must not sell'. Or a less strict duty, a should or a should not: 'In the month of Ab, one reduces joy', 'should reduce'; 'On Purim, women do not wail', 'should not wail'. Or a concession, a may or a need not: 'On Purim, women sing dirges', 'may sing'; 'If a man kills somebody not entitled to be there, he does not go into exile', 'need not go'. There are further possibilities, such as a denial of effect, a cannot: 'The proselyte does not recite the traditional declaration', 'cannot validly recite' seeing it speaks of the land 'promised to our fathers'. Frequently, it is an in-between nuance that prevails; and now and then, indeed, the meaning will remain obscure—for instance, we do not know whether it is may or must.[43]

As already mentioned, this type of guidance acquires currency at some stage between the two Testaments. In fact, it occurs not a single time in the Old nor in any of the ancient Near-Eastern codes, hence must be the Tannaitic lawmaker's response to a fundamental *novum* facing him. This is not hard to identify. It is that immediate revelation has ended, the framework of right living is complete. Legislation by means of 'you shall' or 'you shall not', transmitting the direct will of God, is, therefore, no longer appropriate. The task now is to interpret the old statutes promulgated from on high and to stabilize their execution. The participle of the correct practice as I would call it, 'one does' or 'one does not' in translation, sets out what, on elaboration and systematization of the Scriptural material, emerges as the commendable course. (In a way, the development corresponds to one in the domain of worship—from

---

[42] Manual of Discipline 1.18, 20, 2.11, 18.

[43] For similar difficulties where the imperfect is employed, see my *Collaboration with Tyranny in Rabbinic Law*, 1965, pp. 95 ff.

spontaneous Psalm to derivative Benediction.) It is the learned student of the holy text who speaks in 'The proselyte brings the firstfruits but does not recite the declaration', the guardian and organizer of ritual in every sphere who speaks in 'On Purim, women sing dirges but do not wail'. The sober tone, the limitless range, the fluidity in nuances, all chime with such *au fond* secondary activity. The connection with *halakha*, 'the walking', the principal Tannaitic term for a recognized ruling, and with *derekh*, 'way', a central term for normative custom,[44] is obvious.

Even a decree by the High Priest John Hyrcanus—second half of the second century B.C.—if we may rely on the version offered by the Gemara, is couched in this fashion: 'He who buys fruits from an Uninstructed separates first tithe and second tithe'. For, however authoritative, it is subsidiary to Biblical law. Its aim is somewhat to make up for the widespread laxity of common folks in paying their dues and, indeed, it forms part of a perennial search of the leaders for solutions at once satisfying the scrupulous and not imposing too heavy a burden. It is a question, not of a divine command, but of working out, under such a command, the proper route to take. I might add that my argument would be scarcely affected should the phrasing before us be unauthentic: it would still be what the Rabbis thought plausible in an edict of this kind.

We can probe deeper. It would have been open to the Tannaites, while avoiding 'you shall', 'you shall not', to resort to a straight 'do', 'do not' (the Hebrew imperative being relatively mild—I shall come back to this[45]) or to a circumlocution like 'it is needful to do so-and-so', 'meritorious', 'forbidden', 'permissible'. These all are quite suitable for derivative provisions and they do indeed occupy a far from negligible place in Tannaitic sources. What is there about 'ones does', 'one does not', that makes it a successful competitor?

Its characteristic, we saw, is the setting forth of a precept as a fact or, to put it negatively, the absence of any reference to obligation such as marks the other styles I have adduced, 'you shall', 'you shall not', 'do', 'do not', 'it is meritorious', 'it is forbidden'. Needless to say, a system of duties is presupposed even in concessions like 'you may', 'it is permissible', granting relief. None of all this in 'one does' or 'one does not'. A simple datum—yet it

---

[44] Cp. my remarks in *Festschrift Fritz Schulz*, 1951, vol. 1, pp. 140 ff.
[45] See below, pp. 91 ff.

constrains or exempts no less than those overt prescriptions. To understand the Tannaitic predilection for it, we have to solve this mystery, the acquisition of directive import by an observation.

This occurs because the pattern is meant for an élite—better, for a body believing itself to be an élite: with what justification does not matter. An élite requires only to be informed of the proper behaviour to act accordingly. The implication is: 'In a community as superior as this one, such-and-such is done', 'not done', 'all right if desired', 'not *de rigeur*'. No need for 'must', 'must not' and so on. Indeed, anything smacking of compulsion would be out of place. 'Dinner jacket is worn', an invitation to All Souls College will say. Wherever the form is genuinely applied (by 'genuinely' I mean not by way of completely dried-up routine) this is the spirit behind it. 'A boy, or a brave boy, does not cry' appeals to the youngster's pride in being among that choice part of the human species, boys or brave boys. What endows the factual description of a custom with regulatory effect is the addressee's desire to belong to the nobility singled out by this bearing.

There is plenty of confirmative evidence. The etymology of the designation *perushim*, 'Pharisees', is uncertain; but doubtless it was widely taken to denote 'those keeping apart'. What is of direct relevance is that quite a few rules which ended up binding on the whole people demonstrably began as conventions of a select body. It was the company of Associates that engaged to comply with the minutiae of tithes and cleanness, and this original circumscription still comes through in the Mishnah: 'He who undertakes to be an Associate does not sell an Uninstructed produce and does not receive him if he wears his ordinary garment'. Again, the Qumran Manual stipulates that, when new members are being received, 'The priests recount the just exploits of God and the levites recount the iniquities of the children of Israel and all that enter confess after them'.[46] This never became the general law, but the form recurs in the Tannaitic norms concerning the reception of a convert: 'And two scholars stand by his side and inform him of lighter and heavier commandments'.[47]

Significantly, Amoraic authors evince far less partiality for the participle of the correct practice. By their time, Pharisaism has long

---

[46] Manual 1.18 ff.
[47] Babylonian Yebamoth 47b.

ceased to be an affair of an élite. It is orthodox doctrine: the pattern continues but, except for special contexts, in a subdued mode.

On the other hand, in the earliest Christian communities, it does have its full function. It is met in Paul and the First Epistle of Peter. Paul: 'One abhors the evil, one prefers one another in honour'.[48] Peter: 'The servants subject themselves to their masters'.[49] If you look up the Greek, you will find it quite ungrammatical. What has happened is that primitive Christian canons which were in Hebrew and used the participle—our present—have been overliterally done into Greek. Even the auxiliary is omitted, good Hebrew but impossible Greek, so that we get: 'Abhorring (in the plural) the evil, preferring (plural) one another', 'The servants subjecting themselves'—not 'They are abhorring, preferring', 'The servants are subjecting themselves', just *apostogountes, proegomenoi*. New Testament scholars, perplexed, when translating, usually substitute an imperative: 'Abhor, prefer', 'Be subject'. This is understandable but, besides covering up the genesis of the texts, it falsifies their particular note. Imperative and 'one does' or 'one does not' represent very different types of authority. The maxims before us emphasize the specialness of the new fellowship.

It used to be thought that the sections detailing Christian conduct in which these oddly phrased admonitions are found were the work of Paul and that the First Epistle of Peter borrowed from him: it has indeed been a major argument against Peter's authorship of this Epistle. In reality, each independently draws on Hebrew codes of the sect. Otherwise, I Peter would surely echo Paul also outside these ordinances, but it does not. Moreover, though its Greek is generally better than Paul's, several times it uses the un-Greek participle for a norm appearing in decent Greek in Paul. The latter instructs slaves in the imperative: 'Servants, obey the masters', *hypakouete*.[50] Peter would not have substituted the Hebrew form: it must derive from the source common to both. Whether they themselves are responsible for the Greek or whether, when they wrote, there already were Greek versions in circulation I leave open.

---

[48] Romans 12.9 f.
[49] I Peter 2.18.
[50] Ephesians 6.5, Colossians 3.22—assuming that at least Colossians is authentic.

That this haughty style is taken over by a movement one of whose major complaints about the dominant circles is their arrogance[51] is not without irony—tragic irony:[52] the truth is that a band trying to provide a model to the ordinary world around it cannot but consider itself better, in some respects at any rate. Of course, meekness being a chief virtue, 'one does' or 'one does not' can be adopted only in unawareness of its character. As I pointed out in discussing the choice between 'if' and 'whoever',[53] form, unlike substance, tends to be fastened on by instinct rather than deliberation—hence it often lets us in on unavowed attitudes. In the case of the structure under notice, this happens again and again. No one keener on we-are-all-the-same than the scouts. Yet paragraph 2 of the Scouts Law opens, 'A Scout is loyal to the King', paragraph 4, 'A Scout is a friend to all'. They would have spotted no incongruity in a further one: 'A Scout is humble'.

In passing, contemporary ads are by way of turning from depiction—realistic or fictitious—to prescription. 'Top executives use Lilac Waft deodorant'. (Captain—first world war—Cyril Falls, for many years military correspondent of the Times and attached to All Souls, once remarked to me: 'I'll be damned if I get rid of my smell'. A gentleman of the old school.) 'Successful women buy Gucci shoes'. Not quite yet on a level with the conventions of the Associates, but pushing that way. Negatives are rare in this domain, chiefly because you must not openly run down competitors—'A lady does not wear a Woolworth hat'—also, you do not wish to offend that part of the public who, as yet, are unconverted. Still, 'The expert jogger does not wear sandals' or 'Thoughtful parents do not try to take the place of the Ultimate Lurch therapist with their children' is possible.

Once we grasp the tenor of the participle, we shall not be surprised never to find it with a basic, universal law. A precept 'One does not kill' is unthinkable in Rabbinic speech. This interdict is not a special restraint worked out for observance by the faithful. It is different when we come to the problem under what conditions it is or is not in order to kill a man about to commit a sin: 'These one

---

[51] Romans 2.19, 10.3.

[52] John Noonan, to whom I submitted the typescript, comments: 'not too tragic, just natural'. He is right, and my appraisal is a hangover from my falsely perfectionist upbringing.

[53] See above, p. 74.

saves at the cost of their lives—he that pursues after his fellow to slay him or after a male to force him into intercourse; but he that pursues after a beast or profanes the Sabbath, one does not save them at the cost of their lives'.[54] Here the concern is with details of this particular system. Similarly, we would not say in English, 'One does not kill', 'A boy does not kill', though we might say, 'One does not shoot a defenceless enemy', 'A boy imbued with Zen does not volunteer for combatant service'. Naturally, all depends on the individual culture. In the Rabbinic one, 'One does not blaspheme God', 'One does not commit adultery', 'One does not steal', 'One does not have homosexual relations', are almost as inconceivable as 'One does not kill'. Today, at least 'One does not blaspheme God' would readily pass, intended for an elevated milieu. Similar formulations for the other three lapses would make sense in California, and even 'One does not kill' may not be far off.

A striking Roman illustration of the pattern is furnished by the set of taboos which, according to Gellius,[55] must be heeded by a priest of Jupiter. Many of them are in the present indicative: 'He has no knot in his headdress', 'He does not pass under slips trained upwards from vines', 'If he loses his wife, he abdicates his office'. I am aware that the verbal fidelity of Gellius's quotes cannot be proved. But for my purpose it suffices that an antiquarian of the middle of the second century A.D., and most likely also his source Fabius Pictor, of the middle of the second century B.C.,[56] looked on this form as appropriate for the statutes of a high-ranking fraternity.

Of 'you shall' or 'you shall not', I said above that, though at first sight it seems sanctionless, this appearance is deceptive. Its meaning shades off into 'you will' or 'you will not', hence anyone disobeying removes himself from God-ordained destiny, is lost.[57] If we fully take in the élitist setting of the form here analysed, it, too, turns out far less tame than it looks. It states no penalty for transgression; indeed, it totally refrains from coercive language, it merely describes the distinctive customs of a group. Yet by doing so, it also defines who is and who is not a member. When you reprimand your lad, 'A boy does not cry', then, if he does, he proves not to be

---

[54] Mishnah Sanhedrin 8.7.
[55] Gellius, *Attic Nights* 10.15.9, 13, 22.
[56] Not the more famous third century B.C. annalist.
[57] See above, p. 75.

a true boy. The Tannaitic pattern, as I have tried to show, implies: 'In a community as superior as this one, such-and-such is done or not done'. It follows, logically, that if you flout the rule, you are not inside. 'In the month of Ab, one reduces—literally, they are reducing—joy'. If you have fun instead, you are not designated by 'one', you do not belong to 'them', you fall outside that special crowd. 'An Associate does not sell an Uninstructed produce'; if you do sell, you are not a proper Associate. 'A priest of Jupiter has no knot in his headdress', 'A Scout is a friend to all'; a gallant sporting a rococo coiffure is not a genuine priest of Jupiter, a mean guy is not a real scout. An old division of norms is into *lex perfecta*, announcing a punishment to be inflicted on a transgressor, and *lex imperfecta*, with no such threat. The participle of the correct practice is something of a *lex perfectissima*. Beneath its peaceful semblance lurks an automatic retribution of ultimate severity, exactly the kind suited to an élite, than which nothing worse can befall a person: exclusion from the club.

The most widely remembered New Testament form of promulgation is, I guess, 'you have heard but I say', in the sermon on the mount,[58] attached to five or six topics: murder, adultery, oath, insulting blows, love of fellow-humans and, maybe, divorce though the phrasing is here abridged.[59] 'You have heard that it was said...thou shalt not kill and whosoever shall kill shall be in danger of the judgment. But I say unto you, that whosoever is angry with his brother shall be in danger of the judgment'.

Superficially, this sounds as if the old dispensation were being completely overthrown. At once, however, we come up against the introductory assurance, 'I am not come to destroy but to uphold'.[60] One might perhaps try to brush it aside. It is plainly later than what it prefaces: you do not protest your innocence unless accused. The teachings must have been coined first, they were branded as impious by the establishment who felt menaced, and to this 'I am not come' and so on makes reply. How much of the development took place in Jesus's lifetime and how much afterwards I need not here work out. What matters is the relative posteriority of the opening

---

[58] Matthew 5.21 ff. See the magisterial work by W. D. Davies, *The Setting of the Sermon on the Mount*, 1964, pp. 101 ff., 235 ff., 300 f.
[59] Matthew 5.31 f.
[60] On 'uphold', Hebrew *qiyyem*, as the most plausible rendering, see my *The New Testament and Rabbinic Judaism*, 1956, repr. 1973, pp. 60 f.

summary: at first sight, it might appear arguable that, for the purpose of defence, it tones down an original, extremist object of the pronouncements. But that this is not so, that, on the contrary, it offers an absolutely correct assessment, emerges when we inspect the form in question more closely.

No doubt, it has a majestic ring and I shall come back to it. But to a Jewish audience of the time, the contrast between hearing and saying, more precisely, between what the Torah is heard to declare and what it should be said to declare, is quite familiar and betokens not an annulment of the heard by the said but a refinement: an initial crude understanding—what is heard—is being rectified—so as to become what must be said. On the notice in Exodus that 'the Lord came down on mount Sinai', Rabbi Judah the Prince comments:[61] 'I might hear this as it is heard, but you must say, If the sun, one of the many servants of God, may remain in its place and nevertheless be effective beyond it, how much more He by whose word the world came into being'. To our critical intelligence it is obvious that the Biblical author does have in mind an actual descent of God and few of us will be worried: why should he be less primitive than Hammurabi or Homer? In a sense, then, the Rabbi is repudiating the Pentateuch's theology in favour of one more advanced. Yet this is not how he sees it. For him, whatever the *prima facie* tenor of a text, if we only search deep enough, taking account of all we know in every field, its true meaning will prove to accord with the most ideal standards. In other words, these are never adopted at the expense of Scripture; rather, they are always pointed to by it. The term 'to uphold' is conspicuous in this kind of interpretation. Rabbi Akiba and one Pappos debate Job's remark about God: 'He is apart and who can turn him?'[62] Against Pappos, who finds God here represented as judging with no regard to right or wrong, Akiba 'upholds' the verse by contending that it stresses the irrevocability of a divine sentence without in the least denying its supreme fitness.

The series 'you have heard but I say' has close affinity with the Rabbinic approach. Alas, a modern public may find this hard to accept as far as two of the six topics are concerned. I start with the

---

[61] Mekhilta on Exodus 19.20.
[62] Mekhilta on Exodus 14.29, referring to Job 23.13. See W. Bacher, *Die Exegetische Terminologie der Jüdischen Traditionsliteratur*, Part I, Tannaiten, 1899, pp. 170 f.; *Die Agada der Tannaiten*, vol. 1, 2nd ed., 1903, pp. 318 f.

four easy ones. The Decalogue condemns murder—if we ponder law and prophets thoroughly (such is the thought behind its treatment in the sermon) this must include ill-will; adultery—this must include ill-lust; false oath—this must include any dragging down of the sacred; and the commandment to love your neighbour, in view of all else the Bible puts before us, must include love of your enemy. With insulting blows and divorce, things are more complicated. Scriptural law, as understood in Jesus's time,[63] imposes a fine on assault; the sermon on the mount enjoins the utmost meekness on the victim. Scriptural law recognizes divorce, the sermon rejects it. In these cases, is there not an open break with the former religion? Well, not from the then prevailing point of view. The Rabbis manage to reconcile the boldest innovations with sacred writ—by assuming, for instance, that a certain regulation found there constitutes a concession for the mass but ought not to be taken advantage of by the truly devout; and they always discover somewhere in the Bible a text which, they believe, bears them out. Some of them disapprove of private ownership, claiming that insistence on it is depicted in the Book of Genesis as typical of Sodom.[64] Many are opposed to polygamy, and they cite in their support the God-created union between Adam and Eve.[65] Among sects like the Essenes, deviation construed as following out the essential intent of the revealed word is, of course, even more pronounced. Evidently, up to a point, the relation between hearing and saying throughout the proclamations here discussed corresponds to that found in the Tannaitic sources.

Still, it is up to a point only: there are enormous differences. For one thing, the deeper demands taking off from, and contrasted with, the literal ones are all distinctly uncompromising. Further, the very listing of five to six such antitheses one after another—unparalleled in the Talmud—introduces a somewhat revolutionary tone. Again, the form itself alludes to a new eon. I have not so far mentioned that twice—in connection with murder and oath—a brief clause is added: the proclamation begins not simply 'you have

---

[63] See my *The New Testament and Rabbinic Judaism*, 1956, repr. 1973, pp. 254 ff.

[64] Mishnah Aboth 5.10, doubtless based on Genesis 14.21 ff. See my lecture in *Journal of Jewish Studies*, vol. 10, 1959, p. 5.

[65] Aboth de-Rabbi Nathan 2.5a, referring to Genesis 2.21 ff. and Job 31.1. See my *The New Testament and Rabbinic Judaism*, p. 77, and *Journal of Jewish Studies*, vol. 10, 1959, p. 6.

heard that it was said' but 'you have heard that it was said to them of old time'. Surely, the implication is that the immature grasp, to be expected from those groping novices, is not tolerable in the Christian world.

But even the central portion of the form diverges significantly from the Rabbinic model. The latter's setting is scholarly reflection or interchange. The above-quoted passage about God on mount Sinai begins, 'I might hear this as it is heard', the sage talking to himself; and it goes on, 'but you must say', more precisely, 'but thou must say' (the Hebrew employs the singular), directed to an imaginary fellow-sage or disciple. Moreover, this 'but thou must say' is followed, not directly by the right solution, but by a consideration leading up to it; not, that is, by a categorical 'God's descent was not corporeal' but by 'Since the sun, a mere servant of God, may act in the distance without moving, clearly God may'. By contrast, the teachings in the sermon start off with a rebuking 'you have heard', addressed to the multitude. Then comes—still addressed to them—a sovereign 'but I say unto you', and it enunciates the true understanding, not a ground for regarding it as such: 'Whoever is angry with his brother shall be in danger of the judgment'. I discount some vestigial argumentation in the ban on swearing—'neither by heaven, for it is God's throne' etc.—and also, of course, appended reasoning—like 'for if you salute your brethren only, what do you more than others?'.

By now you may be fed up with my to and fro, but I shall not apologize: the form expresses the New Testament's complex attitude to the Torah. The latter is of no avail or even injurious if narrowly construed, turned into a tight, arid regime. It is still valid, and only valid, if deference is paid to its ultimate, generous goals, if 'your righteousness exceeds that of the scribes and Pharisees'. No wonder once this alive, open course is radically pursued, things will no longer be the same as before, to the dismay of conservative circles. The answer given them, 'I am not come to destroy but to uphold', is, however, quite genuine: the visionaries are convinced—just like, say, Hillel, Johanan ben Zaccai, the Dead Sea faction—that theirs is the proper insight into the meaning of Scripture.

Here I have to recall yet one more point—a negative finding already adverted to: the New Testament never (save in quotations) employs 'you shall' or 'you shall not'. Absent friends can be as conspicuous as present ones[66] and, in this case, neglect of this experience has definitely caused confusion. That the mode of ordinance impressing God's will directly on the individual is entirely missing has weighty implications. Before going further, let me rule out the possibility that the form did once figure in Jesus's preaching and got lost through a vagary of transmission. We may safely assume that, had it occurred anywhere in early Christian tradition, it would have been treasured as a symbol of his supremacy; indeed, it would soon have crept into sayings not originally containing it. The fact is that Jesus is not, in form, presenting another Sinaitic revelation. Admittedly, it is conceivable that a centuries-old reverential instinct would prevent the use of the pattern even after his recognition as the Messiah, a second Moses, Godlike. But even on this basis, there remains something in 'you shall', 'you shall not', too mighty, too awesome, to be transferred.

Once we are aware of this absence, it is in fact particularly striking in the sermon. After 'you have heard thou shalt not kill, but I say unto you', the natural continuation would be 'thou shalt not be angry with thy brother'. Instead, there is almost—from the formal angle—an anticlimax: 'that whosoever is angry with his brother shall be in danger of the judgment', reminiscent—as to form—of a statement like Eleazar of Modiim's (he was Bar Kokhba's uncle):[67] 'He who...puts his fellow to shame in public has no share in the world to come'. This structure, too, would be worth exploring; here it suffices to observe that, compared with 'you shall' or 'you shall not', it is sober, grading, classifying. In the same way, 'thou shalt not commit adultery' is followed not by 'thou shalt not look on a woman to lust' but by 'whosoever looks to lust has already committed adultery in his heart': in form, mere exegesis determining the scope of the statute, the act furthest from the central one still falling under it (in a sense at least[68]). Again, to 'thou shalt not forswear thyself' it would be simple to oppose 'thou shalt not swear at all'. What we actually find is 'but I say unto you not to swear at all': a very subdued, dependent infinitive—as in the counsel against exacting satisfaction, 'but I say unto you not to

---

[66] Cp. my remark on Gideon in *Typologie im Werk des Flavius Josephus* (Bayerische Akademie der Wissenschaften, Philos.-Histor. Klasse, Sitzungsberichte, Heft 6), 1977, p. 24, English transl. *Journal of Jewish Studies*, vol. 31, 1980, p. 33.

[67] Mishnah Aboth 3.12.

[68] See my lecture in *Natural Law Forum*, vol. 12, 1967, pp. 49 f.

resist evil'. A little further on in the part about oath, 'neither mayest thou swear by thy head', *me* with the subjunctive, comes closer to 'thou shalt not', which makes the avoidance of the final step all the more impressive. Lastly, 'thou shalt love thy neighbour' is widened not, into 'thou shalt love thine enemy' but into 'love your enemies'. This is an imperative with a strong Wisdom component—like 'Love the truth' in the Testament of the Twelve Patriarchs.[69] 'Turn the other cheek', too, belongs here. I shall say something about this form in a moment.

Translations, form-blind, give us 'you shall' or 'you shall not' quite freely. German, French and other versions adopt an analogous course. In some cases it may not be easy to hit on a pleasing alternative but in others it is. A reverse aberration is found in The New English Bible, in the creation of which my admired friend C. H. Dodd played the leading role. It eliminates 'you shall' and 'you shall not', substituting: 'Do not commit murder', 'do not commit adultery', 'do not break your oath'. The Ten Commandments defanged.

For completeness's sake: the farewell talk of Jesus in John, though inculcating 'a new commandment', *entole kaine*, shows no trace of 'you shall' or 'you shall not'. 'A new commandment I give unto you, that you love one another'.[70] A sage's distilled conclusion, the all-important task he bequeathes which embraces all other tasks, stated solemnly yet quietly, without any break in the didactic mood. The New English Bible cannot bear having the sublime teaching in a subordinate clause. It puts, 'I give you a new commandment: love one another'. It sounds alright, at a price: the injection of a separate imperative dissipates the original atmosphere.

Do not get me wrong. Had I been on the Dodd-Committee, I would have pointed out the distortions but not, necessarily, have voted against them. A modern version for general use has to strike a balance between accuracy and appeal. This may be the place for a reminiscence. When Dodd was asked to direct the huge project, he discussed with me how to decide. For a considerable time before, he had talked to me about a Life of Jesus as his crowning work. I was very keen on his accomplishing this and, mindful of his fairly recent bout of tuberculosis, was not wholeheartedly in favour of another

---

[69] Testament of Reuben 3.9.
[70] John 13.34.

commitment that would engage him for several years. (My brother died of T.B.) But he felt strongly that the Bible should be freshly translated for each generation and that participation in this enterprise was a more urgent calling than anything else. He did see the translation through and he did write The Founder of Christianity.[71]

To sum up. In the Old Testament form, God's voice compels the individual conscience;[72] obedience means hope, disregard utter ruin. The Tannaitic participle constitutes a painstaking working out of the way of life an élite will pursue on the basis of the hallowed documents. And the antitheses of the sermon on the mount stand in between, representing a fresh impulse on the one hand, a faithful acceptance of the traditional framework on the other.

At this juncture, we might look at the Fifth Commandment—at least I first heard of it as no. 5—'Honour your father and your mother' etc., or, to imitate the Hebrew singular, 'Honour thy father and thy mother'. Here we meet an imperative, which I labelled above as gentler than 'you shall' or 'you shall not'.[73] In fact, with one dubious exception, it is the only ordinance in the Pentateuch couched in this mood. Commentators slur over the difference from the Sabbath-Commandment, with an infinitive: 'To remember the Sabbath day'.[74] But though the infinitive is closer to the imperative than to 'you shall', 'you shall not', it is not the same.

The Rabbis see a bidding to marry and beget children in the words God addresses to Adam and Eve, Noah and his sons and Jacob: 'Be fruitful and multiply'.[75] In reality, they are just a blessing, with not the remotest intention of imposing a duty, legal, moral or religious—as when Jethro releases Moses with 'go in peace',[76] or when we say 'farewell', 'be well', 'enjoy yourselves', 'have a good day'. Exactly the same words are used when fish and fowl have been created;[77] and the Bible itself speaks of a blessing in both cases, men and animals.[78] The Rabbinic reinterpretation dates from the era of Augustus. Even then it is not whole-hearted,

---

[71] We now have a discerning biography of Dodd by F. W. Dillistone, 1977.
[72] See Excursus 2, below, pp. 123 ff.
[73] See above, pp. 75, 81, 91.
[74] Thus, G. Beer, *Exodus*, 1959, p. 100: *Inf. abs.* = *Imptv.*
[75] Genesis 1.28, 9.1, 7, 35.11, Genesis Rabba ad 1, Mishnah Yebamoth 6.6.
[76] Exodus 4.18.
[77] Genesis 1.22.
[78] Genesis 1.22, 28, 9.1.

but its consequences in the next two millennia have been tremendous.[79]

What about a number of injunctions accompanied by a warning like 'guard this', 'guard yourself'? 'Guard that which I command you, guard yourself lest you make a covenant with the inhabitant of the land'.[80] These imperatives do not, like 'Honour your father', convey the substance of the legislation: in the example just cited, the actual law is clearly the ban on a treacherous covenant, 'lest you make'. They are stereotype, cautionary introductions or closings of a statute with a view to stressing its importance—not to mention the fact that their ultimate provenance overlaps with that of the substantial 'Honour'.

There are, of course, a great many imperatives in orders for the individual, momentary occasion. God calls on Abraham, 'Go from your land',[81] or on Moses, 'Speak to the children of Israel';[82] Judah decides to have Tamar put to death, 'Bring her forth and she shall be burnt'.[83] These instructions can be quite comprehensive. Abraham, for instance, is exhorted, 'Walk before me and be perfect'.[84] But it is still not lawmaking for the people at large and valid for future times as well as the present: the reference is exclusively to his personal conduct. Here and there, at first sight, an imperative may look like a law proper, but the impression is deceptive. An invocation like 'hear'—'Hear, o Israel, the Lord is our God'[85]—is always in the Pentateuch confined to the particular audience, quite apart from the fact that it is cautionary emphasis resembling 'guard', 'guard yourself', rather than substance. Or take the passage: 'And now, write you this song and teach it to the children of Israel that it may be a witness for me'.[86] The opening 'and now' shows that what is being demanded is not continuous transmission throughout the generations—as, say, in the law 'and these words which I command you this day shall be in your heart and you shall teach them to your children and you shall write them

---

[79] See my *The New Testament and Rabbinic Judaism*, 1956, repr. 1973, p. 78; *The Duty of Procreation*, 1977, pp. 2 ff., 34 ff.
[80] Exodus 34.11 f.; cp. Deuteronomy 4.9, 12, 28, 24.8.
[81] Genesis 12.1.
[82] Exodus 25.2.
[83] Genesis 38.24.
[84] Genesis 17.1.
[85] Deuteronomy 6.4.
[86] Deuteronomy 31.19.

on the doorposts of your houses'.⁸⁷ The imperative asks for one definite action only: God inspires Moses to a last hymn he is to set down and pass on. A subsequent verse records that the order was executed: 'And Moses wrote this song on that day and taught it the children of Israel'.⁸⁸

The only exception occurs earlier on in the same chapter: 'At the end of every seven years', says Moses to the priests and elders, 'you shall (thou shalt, literally) read this Torah before all Israel; gather (gather thou) the people together that they may hear and learn'.⁸⁹ Obviously, true legislation, and none the less the imperative 'gather'. I suspect it is due partly to the influence of 'gather' in similar contexts where, however, it expresses a special order,⁹⁰ and partly to the legislator putting himself in the situation at the end of each septennial when the time for the reading has arrived and the imperative would fit. It may be worth noting that the portion from 'gather' onward has been held interpolated because, logically, it ought to come before 'you shall read': first, the summons to assemble, then the recital.⁹¹ However, this strikes me as over-critical.

We are left, then, with a unique—or, if you prefer, near-unique—statutory imperative in the Fifth Commandment. Maybe I shall now be told that *kabbedh*, 'honour', could be construed as an infinitive. This would give us 'To honour your father and your mother', analogous to 'To remember the Sabbath day'. To this, I have a fivefold repartee. First, it would be unfair, simply because I have laboriously demonstrated the strangeness of a usage, to explain it away. Up to now, everybody has been happy with an imperative here. Secondly, as already hinted, the original settings of the normative imperative and infinitive have anyhow much in common. Thirdly, this infinitive itself, if we discount routine warnings, 'to remember', 'to guard', figures only about half a dozen times in the Pentateuch. It is so rare that some scholars account for 'To remember the Sabbath day' by calling in the even rarer imperative: 'to remember' equals 'remember'.⁹² Fourthly, the law speaks not of 'father and mother' but of 'your father and your mother'; not, in-

---

⁸⁷ Deuteronomy 6.6 ff.
⁸⁸ Deuteronomy 31.22.
⁸⁹ Deuteronomy 31.10 ff.
⁹⁰ Deuteronomy 4.10, 31.28.
⁹¹ C. Steuernagel, *Deuteronomium und Josua*, 1910, pp. 111 f.
⁹² See G. Beer, *l.c.*

deed, impossible after 'to honour' but going better with the direct address, 'honour'. (The Sabbath Commandment starts off impersonally: 'To remember the Sabbath day to keep it holy'.) Lastly, *kabbedh* recurs in Proverbs, 'Honour the Lord with your substance',[93] paired off with unmistakable imperatives, 'Trust (*beṭaḥ*) in the Lord', 'Fear (*yeraʾ*) the Lord'.[94]

It is time to ask: First, why is the imperative missing from the codes? Second, what brings it into the Fifth Commandment?

As for question 1, the grammatical unsuitability of this mood for prohibitions may come to mind: you cannot in Hebrew say 'Murder not'—a limitation parallelled in many languages. This no doubt excludes it from a huge area. But there remains a mass of positive provisions, never imperatival. Mostly, they use the future—technically, the imperfect—and as a law apparently cannot open with a simple imperfect, we find two varieties. Either the law opens with an imperfect preceded by the infinitive: 'To tithe you shall tithe your produce',[95] 'To furnish you shall furnish your slave when you release him'.[96] The usual rendering is by means of 'surely': 'You shall surely tithe', 'you shall surely furnish'. What interests here is that no quirk of grammar would have prevented an imperative: 'Tithe your produce', 'Furnish your slave'. Or the law places the imperfect at the end: 'My Sabbaths you shall guard and my sanctuaries you shall fear'.[97] Here, too, an imperative would have been quite feasible. At the close of Ecclesiastes, precisely these two verbs appear: 'God fear and his commandments guard'.[98] Another frequent phrasing is for a provision to begin with what a layman might look on as a substitute future, technically, the perfect with the consecutive 'and' (*waw*): 'And you shall offer a lamb',[99] 'And you shall count from the morrow of the Sabbath',[100] 'And you shall love the Lord'.[101] Once again, no grammatical obstacle to an imperative. 'Eat of my bread and drink of the wine I have

---

[93] Proverbs 3.9.
[94] Proverbs 3.5, 7.
[95] Deuteronomy 14.22.
[96] Deuteronomy 15.14.
[97] Leviticus 19.30.
[98] Ecclesiastes 12.13.
[99] Leviticus 23.12.
[100] Leviticus 23.15.
[101] Deuteronomy 6.5.

mingled', we are admonished in Proverbs, 'forsake the foolish and live and go in the way of understanding'.[102]

Perhaps you expect me to say something about the jussive-imperfect with *ʾal* which, much like *me phoneuses* in Greek or *ne occideris* in Latin, serves in the place of a negative imperative, and which does turn up—however sparingly—in the codes. This would lead too far afield, however, and in any case I must leave something for my next visit.

So I proceed to my solution: where it is a question of a rule as opposed to an order on a specific occasion, the Hebrew imperative is far weaker than 'you shall'. It counsels, recommends, rather than imposes, compels. It is common in Wisdom: 'Refrain your foot from the path of the sinners',[103] 'If you have become surety, deliver yourself as a roe from the hunter',[104] 'My son, hear the instruction of your father and forsake not (jussive with *ʾal*) the teaching of your mother'.[105] This is effective education of the young by the old, but it is not the spirit of Pentateuchic legislation, inescapable, the will of God.

And now question no. 2. If, none the less, this mood does surface in 'Honour your father and your mother', it is because the Fifth Commandment descends from Wisdom. To avoid misunderstandings, let me say at once that it need not therefore be later or less devoutly religious than the proper statutes. True, the latter are commonly held to antedate the Wisdom collections—Ecclesiastes, Proverbs and so on—but there was Wisdom among the Hebrews long before these. No one living where they did could have escaped it. Again, the notion of Wisdom—Hebrew Wisdom, in particular—as this-worldly, with little more than lip-service to the divine, has long been seen to be mistaken.[106]

At any rate, the result of form analysis chimes with the contents of the injunction. Respect of the child for the parent is a foremost concern of Oriental Wisdom. The Egyptian Vizier Pta-Hotep opines, 'How good is it when a son accepts what his father says';[107] and I have just adverted to Proverbs, 'My son, hear the instruction

---

[102] Proverbs 9.5 f.
[103] Proverbs 1.15.
[104] Proverbs 6.5.
[105] Proverbs 1.8.
[106] See W. Zimmerli, in H. Ringgren and W. Zimmerli, *Sprüche/Prediger*, 1962, pp. 132 ff., and my article in *Orita*, vol. 3, 1969, p. 51.
[107] See *Ancient Near Eastern Texts*, ed. J. B. Pritchard, 1950, p. 414.

of your father' and so on. What enormously enhances the role of the theme in Wisdom circles is the fact that the father-son relation is the model for the master-disciple one. Think how often the sage addresses his listener 'my son'.

There is a further link to Wisdom. The Fifth Commandment—as noticed in the Epistle to the Ephesians[108]—holds out a reward: in Exodus, 'that your days may be long', in Deuteronomy, 'that your days may be long and that it may be well with you'. That piety is beneficial is a characteristic Wisdom idea. In fact, Wisdom is keen on precisely these benefits, long life and well-being. 'He that is wise attains old age', we are assured in a Babylonian anthology of bilingual adages.[109] The above-quoted line from Proverbs, 'Honour the Lord with your substance', continues 'so shall your barns be filled'. The Psalmist sings: 'What man is he that desires life, loves days to see good? Keep your tongue from evil, depart from evil and do good, seek peace and pursue it'.[110] The Wisdom background of this section at least of the psalm is evident not only from the imperatival maxims but also from their introduction in the preceding verse: 'Come, children, hearken unto me, I will teach you the fear of the Lord'.

Twentieth-century critics postulate the same short *Urform* for each paragraph of the Decalogue: 'it is manifest', *es liegt auf der Hand*, that the reference to reward is an accretion.[111] If all they meant were that in the evolution of Hebrew—or any—society, the duty of filial deference is enunciated before a detailed return for it, I would have no complaint. In fact, I would go further: on this basis, the opening word 'honour' is secondary compared with 'your father and your mother'. However, what they have in mind, of course, is not the sequence in which the various concepts grew up in communal thought but the history of the specific text before us. In the original Decalogue, they claim, it actually ran 'Honour your father and your mother', period; later, it was provided with an appendix, mentioning a douceur. This I cannot accept. The promise hails from the same milieu as the imperative. They are both integral elements of this Wisdom tenet, complementing one another.

---

[108] Ephesians 6.2.
[109] See W. O. E. Oesterley, *The Book of Proverbs*, p. XXXVIII.
[110] Psalms 34.13.
[111] See W. Keszler, *Vetus Testamentum*, vol. 7, 1957, p. 2; G. Beer, *l.c.*; M. Noth, *Das Zweite Buch Moses, Exodus*, 1959, p. 133.

Significantly, in a sense, the promise is unique just like the imperative. E. Würthwein, writing on *misthos*, 'reward', in Theologisches Wörterbuch,[112] observes that pre-Deuteronomic legislation predicts retribution for wrongdoing—'if you do not comply, you will suffer'—but no favours for righteousness—'if you comply, it will be to your advantage'. With certain modifications not here to be set out, this thesis is correct—except for the one case of 'that your days may be long'. Würthwein argues that, really, this clause also announces punishment alone: it has the force of 'if you disobey, you will die young'. Desperate reasoning. By taking this line, we can make a threat of any promise—or vice versa. Your uncle who will pay you a trip to Rome if you pass the exam is really notifying you that that he will withold the cheque if you fail. A law with the death penalty on idolatry is really assuring the orthodox worshipper that he will not be stoned. I am not saying that there are no occasions when such an interpretation may be illuminating, but this is not one of them. We had better admit the irregular positive nature of the long days. Just like the imperative, it is anything but irregular in Wisdom.

While demand and reward thus prove to belong together as primary components of the Fifth Commandment, the latter is something of an erratic block in the code. This should not cause too much surprise: the truth is that, as far as ultimate roots are concerned, we have to do here with a pretty motley compilation. One could not conceive of the Fifth Commandment as originating in the same setting as the Sabbath Commandment, or of either of them in the same as the warnings against murder, adultery and theft. The Rabbis sensed it. In the Noachian world law which they assumed to have been decreed by God after the flood, the Fourth and Fifth Commandments are not represented though murder, adultery and theft are crimes.[113] This is not to underrate the meaningfulness, the marvel, of the Decalogue as a unit, produced at the latest at the moment of promulgation but certainly prepared by earlier developments. Above, in discussing 'you shall' and 'you shall not', I indicated some factors likely to have been decisive in gluing diverse material together. I believe that rather than construct a fan-

---

[112] See E. Würthwein, in *Theologisches Wörterbuch zum Neuen Testament*, ed. G. Kittel, vol. 4, 1942, p. 715. M. Noth, *l.c.* concurs: *Zusage bzw. Warnung*, 'promise, or rather, warning'.

[113] Babylonian Sanhedrin 56a ff.

tastic, homogenized *Urform*, we ought to try to find out more about what led to the achievement of this lasting constitution.

A word on the relation between the Fifth Commandment and Deuteronomy. As Deuteronomy, too, is Wisdom-oriented, it, too, makes much both of the desirable attitude between the generations and of the prizes virtue will bring. But it is palpably later than the Fifth Commandment. The Decalogue appears already in Exodus. Deuteronomy itself depicts its version as a rerun shortly before Moses's death. And in the Fifth Commandment, after 'Honour your father and your mother', it inserts 'as the Lord your God commanded you'. The same insertion is found in the Sabbath Commandment. So with regard to these two, there is additional, specific reference to a prior existence. Is the Fifth Commandment perhaps the product of a trend leading up to Deuteronomy? I doubt it. If it were, surely, Deuteronomy would not be without the imperative.[114] In all probability, the Fifth Commandment and Deuteronomy represent Wisdom streams. There must have been quite a few from early on; and despite the attractiveness of least resistance, it will not do to treat them as identical. As far as the phrasing of norms is concerned, Deuteronomy, as I have shown elsewhere,[115] while not availing itself of the imperative, does contain its own, telling form, midway between advice and ordinary, statutory decree, but I shall not here enlarge on it.

May I, instead, draw your attention to a little point though it is not directly relevant. As remarked above, the inducement of Exodus is 'that your days may be long', to which Deuteronomy adds 'and that it may be well with you'. The expansion may be intended to bring the reward into line with that for not taking a mother bird together with her young ones or her eggs.[116] There is no other law on a specific matter where the combination long days and well-being occurs.[117] In this philosophy, the protection of the mother bird is allied to the Fifth Commandment: we owe piety to parents even in nature. Remember that Deuteronomy prohibits the army, when building siegeworks against a city, from felling a fruitbearing tree for this purpose.[118] That reverence for progenitors

---

[114] On Deuteronomy 31.12, see above, p. 94.
[115] See Orita, vol. 3, 1969, pp. 41 ff.
[116] Deuteronomy 22.6.
[117] Deuteronomy 4.40, 5.30 concerns good conduct in general. Cp. also Psalms 23.6, 34.12 f., 91.16, Proverbs 3.2, 16, Ecclesiastes 8.13.
[118] Deuteronomy 20.19 f.

transcends national boundaries comes out in the statute about a woman taken captive in war whom her captor wishes to marry: she is first to spend a month mourning her—heathen—parents.[119] In one or two of these laws, incidentally, it is motherhood to which homage is paid: Deuteronomy generally advances the status of women.[120]

Here is a pattern produced by the confluence of law and medicine, two spheres which throughout the millennia have interacted in manifold ways. Think of the American Jewish family who want the daughter to marry either a doctor or a lawyer. The form I am going to inspect had puzzled me for years until one night, when I indulged my medical-historical curiosity and browsed in Egyptian medical sources, the connection occurred to me.

Some laws of the Pentateuch are composed of three parts: facts, designation, consequences. Thus, the legislation designed to discriminate between murder and unintentional killing contains this paragraph:[121] 'And if he smote him with an instrument of iron, he is a murderer, the murderer shall surely be put to death'. Part 1 describes the situation, he struck with an iron; 2 subsumes it under a category, he is a murderer; 3 declares what is to happen, he shall be put to death. More precisely, 1 puts the concrete, particular instance, reduced in 2 to its essence, from which follows 3, the verdict applicable to 1. From a narrowly practical point of view, part 2 is superfluous; a court would come to the same decision if it did not exist. The aim is to justify the ruling, to represent it as called for by the logic of the system.

This sequence is met in four chapters only. Besides Numbers 35 about homicide, the following three are pertinent. Leviticus 11, concerning diet: 'The camel (1), because he does not part the hoof (2), he is unclean (3). And every creeping thing (1), it is a detestable thing (2), it shall not be eaten (3)'.[122] Leviticus 13, concerning leprosy: 'And the priest shall see the skin and the hair is turned white (1), it is the plague of leprosy (2), and the priest shall pronounce him unclean (3). and if a man's hair has simply fallen off (1), he is just bald (2), he is clean (3)'.[123] Leviticus 20, concerning

---

[119] Deuteronomy 21.10 ff.
[120] See my illustrations in *Juridical Review*, vol. 90 (n.s. 23), 1978, pp. 177 ff.
[121] Numbers 35.16.
[122] Leviticus 11.4, 41.
[123] Leviticus 13.3, 40.

sexual commerce: 'And a man that lies with a male as with womankind (1), abomination have the two committed (2), they shall surely be put to death, their blood is upon them (3)'.[124]

The statutes are all priestly in character—which is not surprising: the priests were the group most capable of so subtle yet compact a structure. The provenance is obvious for Leviticus 11 and 13, diet and leprosy. But Leviticus 20 also by its contents and language reveals its nature: it suffices to call attention to the prohibition of intercourse with a menstruating woman,[125] and to expressions like 'to uncover the nakedness',[126] 'to uncover the fountain of her blood'.[127] As for the list in Numbers 35, marking off ill-will from inadvertence, it, too, presumably came into existence at some sanctuary when a compromise had to be worked out between its claim and those of the victim's kin or the community.

That echoes of the form are detectable in Ezekiel, 'Ezekiel the priest',[128] supports this finding. 'When I say to the wicked, You shall surely die, and you do not warn him (1), he is wicked (2), he shall die for his iniquity, but his blood I will require at your hand (3)'.[129] Similarly: 'And if a man be just and do law and justice (1), he is just (2), he shall surely live (3)'.[130] The continuation is looser but still influenced by the same model: 'And he begets a son, a robber, who has eaten upon the mountains and defiled his neighbour's wife (1), shall he live?, he shall not live, all these abominations has he done (2), he shall surely die, his blood is upon him (3)'.[131] In a couple of Aramaic papyri, it is true, the style is transferred to the area of contract: 'If she says so, scil. I take away the gift (1), bound she remains (2), she will not be listened to (3)',[132] and again, 'And if he does not do so (1), divorce it is (2), he shall do to her the law of divorce (3)'.[133] Both documents are from the same scribe—a P fan.

What prompted this form? Certain bodies, priests and lawyers above all, from early had the task of making distinctions—the clean

---

[124] Leviticus 20.13.
[125] Leviticus 20.18.
[126] Leviticus 20.11.
[127] Leviticus 20.18.
[128] Ezekiel 1.3.
[129] Ezekiel 3.18.
[130] Ezekiel 18.5 ff.
[131] Ezekiel 18.10 ff.
[132] *Aramaic Papyri of the Fifth Century B.C.*, ed. A. Cowley, 1923, 18.3, p. 55.
[133] *The Brooklyn Museum Aramaic Papyri*, ed. E. G. Kraeling, 1953, 7.38 f., pp. 206 f.

and the unclean, objects fit and unfit for sacrifice, holy and ordinary seasons, the innocent and the guilty, the valid and the void. Gradually, they built up inclusive, coherent orders so that everything might be dealt with in accordance with its classification. In a world where this was the dominant interest, it would be vital, before deciding on a course, to bring the facts under the right heading. Expressed in a form, this meant: facts, heading, decision.

Besides this general background, however, we can discern at least two specific factors. The first has to do with fiction, reinterpretation of narrow norms, irrebuttable evidence and the like. When the provisions laid down for a class are to be extended to facts close to it but outside, it will satisfy an urge for justice, or tidiness, to pronounce them to be within, so that the extension appears well-founded. It is a process constantly going on in legal evolution;[134] to some extent, the current trend of bringing more and more unions under the marriage umbrella furnishes an illustration. In this context, the pattern discussed would be highly appropriate. All five occurrences in the Code of Hammurabi belong here: 'If a man has bought silver or gold from a man's son or slave without witness and bonds, that man is a thief, he shall be put to death'.[135] So does a Hittite paragraph: 'If a member of a guild steals, and the guild do not return the stolen article, they are guilty, all thieves, he (the owner) shall seize them'.[136] Three injunctions in the Laws of Eshnunna seem to owe their tripartite structure to this method of widening a class: 'If a man brought bride money for a man's daughter but another forcibly deflowered her, it is a case of life, he shall die'.[137]

The same urge will be at work if the provisions laid down for a class are to operate whenever certain facts are present though now and then, by way of exception, they do not fall under it: to pronounce them to be within warrants that inflexible operation. The Pentateuch's rule about homicide adduced above is an example: 'If he smote him with an iron, he is a murderer, he shall be put to death'. In nine out of ten cases, the wielder of a deadly weapon is bent on mischief. It is not feasible, at the time, to examine the in-

---

[134] See my article in *Natural Law Forum*, vol. 12, 1967, pp. 25 ff.
[135] Code of Hammurabi 7; cp. 9, 10, 11 and 13. For further aspects, see B. Jackson, *Essays in Jewish and Comparative Legal History*, 1975, pp. 66 ff.
[136] Hittite Laws 49; cp. XXXV.
[137] Laws of Eshnunna 26; cp. 24, 58.

dividual incident as to whether it may constitute the rare abnormality. Hence, if a workable separation of witting and unwitting is to be achieved at all, it can be only a rough-and-ready one. To kill with an iron instrument statistically falls on the wrong side. The law determines—one is tempted to say, explains—that it is murder, and to be punished accordingly. A Hittite parallel: 'If a man seizes a woman in the mountain, the man is wicked, he shall die; but if he seizes her in the house, the woman also is wicked, the woman also shall die'.[138] This regulation is particularly valuable for form analysis since the corresponding Biblical one demonstrates dramatically in how different a fashion the same idea can be conveyed. In Deuteronomy 22, the, irrebuttably assumed, connivance of the girl in one case and struggle in the other are depicted in didactic detail in appendices to the respective verdicts: 'If a damsel is betrothed and a man finds her in the city and lies with her, you shall stone them that they die, the damsel because she cried not and the man because he has humbled his neighbour's wife. But if a man finds a betrothed damsel in the field and lies with her, the man only shall die, but unto the damsel you shall do nothing, there is in the damsel no deadly sin, for he found her in the field and she cried and there was none to save her'.[139] Quite unlike the rigorous tripartite pronouncements.

The second factor that must have played a role I alluded to at the start of this section: it takes us to another branch of civilisation. In the ancient Orient, both Egypt and Babylonia, the main stream of the tripartite directive flows, not in legal codifications, but in medical ones. It is in the latter that the scheme (1) facts, or as we should now say, symptoms, (2) designation, or rather now, diagnosis, (3) consequences, or rather, treatment, is common.[140] 'If a woman has an issue, say: It is the *achat* disease, apply jaspis with honey'.[141] Forty-eight such instructions are met in the Edwin Smith Surgical papyrus alone. A cuneiform specimen runs: 'If his joints are all painful, it is a swollen joint lasting two years, make him rest on leavened meal, with leaven you atone'.[142]

---

[138] Hittite Laws 197.
[139] Deuteronomy 22.23 ff.
[140] See O. Temkin, *Kyklos, Jahrbuch für Geschichte und Philosophie der Medizin*, vol. 3, 1930, pp. 102 ff.
[141] From Papyrus Ebers; see O. Temkin, p. 109.
[142] From *Assyrian Incantation against Rheumatism*; see O. Temkin, p. 127.

In medicine, part 2 is of direct, practical relevance—or at least, has been held to be that—from remotest antiquity to very recent times: treatment must be preceded by diagnosis. There are rational grounds for this and less defensible ones, a mixture which often turns the procedure into a cult. The rational side is stressed by a translator of Hippocrates: 'A modern doctor, when called to a case of illness, is always careful to diagnose it, that is, to put it in its proper place in the catalogue of diseases....Diseases may be similar in symptoms and yet call for different medicines'.[143] But over-reliance on the catalogue is common, to the neglect of the peculiar features of a case—not to mention true empathy with the patient. For ancient doctors, the importance of part 2 is even greater, for two reasons. First, understandably,[144] it not seldom brings out the hopelessness of the condition, so that part 3, treatment, becomes non-treatment: 'this ailment I shall not tend'. Second, even if the sickness appears manageable, at a primitive stage, to conquer it it is thought necessary to discover its name or that of the demon causing it. Maybe more of this belief (even it not without rational ingredients) survives to this day than the profession would care to avow. 'A quacksalver', John Webster writes,[145] 'is a mountebank of a larger bill than a tailor; if he can but come by names enow of diseases to stuff it with, 'tis all the skill he studies for'. At any rate, medicine provides the perfect setting for the sequence of the three parts we are investigating.

The Old Testament statutes about leprosy and food are plainly dealing with questions to some degree of a medical nature; and even the particular chapter about intercourse which contains the form has a faintly medical flavour—remember the tabooing of the menses. This is not to assert that all, or any, of these provisions originated strictly in medical science and from thence invaded religion and law. More probably, they are due to a priestly class dominating both medicine and diverse other fields—sexual behaviour and the granting of asylum among them. Support for this view is furnished by the portion of the Hittite Laws from which I have already quoted the paragraph concerning rape. The pattern occurs here two more times, used exactly as in Leviticus 20:

---

[143] W. H. Jones, *Hippocrates* (Loeb Classical Library), vol. 2, 1943, p. IX.

[144] On how little could be done by medicine till very recently, see L. Thomas, *Bulletin of the American Academy of Arts and Sciences*, vol. 34, no. 1, Oct. 1980, pp. 21 ff.

[145] *Characters*, No. 24, A Quacksalver.

bestiality—an abomination—capital punishment.[146] There are unmistakable signs of priestly contribution to this section: a ghost seems to figure in one paragraph,[147] exclusion from priestly rank is ordained in another,[148] a differentiation is made between a cow, sheep, dog or pig[149] and a horse or mule.[150] At the same time, no medical notions are in evidence. Priestly interest, without explicit pointers to medicine, is discernible, too, in a part of an Assyrian compilation where, possibly, the diagnosis pattern is employed.[151] These parallels indeed suggest that we have to do with a style widespread among Oriental priesthood in an age prior to the Biblical texts.

What does appear certain is that the medical model was a major agent in its genesis and expansion. After all, the connection between disease, sin and crime and between cure, atonement and punishment prevalent in Hebrew thought and throughout the East—not to forget Greece[152]—is frequently commented on; and it is less astonishing that there exists this form shared by medical prescriptions and other priestly norms than that such a link has not been looked for long before now. The wide range of life covered by the pattern reflects the wide range of priestly sway. Who knows?, it may not be the only one of its kind.

As for its extent in space and time—it is not found in Greek, Roman or Germanic legislation. Yet it does emerge now and then in systems specially keen on the sort of logic it represents. The Austrian Penal Code favours it. 'Whoever with intent to kill acts against a man in such a way that this or another man's death results—becomes guilty of the crime of murder—he shall be punished with life imprisonment'. 'Whoever throws into a well, a cistern, a river or a brook the water of which serves a settlement for drinking or brewing dead cattle or anything else by which the water may become dirty or unhealthy—commits an offence—and shall be punished with arrest from three days to one month'.[153] Strangely, it

---

[146] Hittite Laws 187, 188.
[147] Hittite Laws 190.
[148] Hittite Laws 200 A.
[149] Hittite Laws 187 f.
[150] Hittite Laws 200 A.
[151] Middle Assyrian Laws A51; see R. Yaron, *Biblica*, vol. 51, 1970, p. 556.
[152] See above, p. 65.
[153] *Strafgesetz über Verbrechen, Vergehen und Übertretungen* etc., 1852, wiederverlautbart als *Österreichisches Strafgesetz* 1945, 134, 136, 398.

seems to do something for a criminal or a patient to be told that he is being hanged or kept incarcerated for first degree murder or that he is dying from Alibert's Mycosis Fungoides.[154]

My I append an observation respecting another medical arrangement imitated outside medicine though not in law. Once again, the clue lies in its being of distinctly greater, actual utility in connection with medicine.

Technical manuals of classical antiquity often fall into two parts: the technique and the technician.[155] Horace on poetry or Quintilian on rhetoric expounds separately the craft of writing or speaking and the requisite qualities of writer or speaker. It has of course been seen that this division occurs also in medical literature. In my opinion, that is where it arose. In medicine—which I take in a wide sense, including doctors, midwives and the like—the way of life, health, conduct and appearance of the practitioner have an immediate impact on the practice, far more so than in other fields. Mostly, that is, the healer's person is as important as what he does or prescribes. (Admittedly, it is changing now, with the automation of this calling.) So when the work on The Physician attributed to Hippocrates treats of the doctor in chapter one and of tumours in the following ones,[156] or when Soranus of Ephesus discusses first the midwife and then midwifery,[157] the student will benefit in the most practical fashion. I am not denying that the scheme makes sense elsewhere too: in fact, this is the reason for its popularity. But its birthplace is medicine to which it is most directly helpful.

Now and then, it may be possible to link a pattern with a particular school of thought. The Talmudic le'olam seems to be in point: I would call it the Stoic Ever. 'Ever should a man be accustomed to say, Everything that the All-Merciful does he does for the best',[158] 'Never should a man remain in a place of danger and

---

[154] Long after writing this, I come across in the *San Francisco Chronicle* (August 9, 1980, People, p. 11) a tale of an ailment starting in 1970 but receiving its 'differential diagnosis' only in 1978: Sclerodoma plus Sjogren's Syndrome. Treatment—or non-treatment—remains much the same as before, but the patient-narrator is lyrical about the christening: 'My years of agonizing anxiety, despair and emotional trauma are over'.

[155] See E. Norden, *Hermes*, vol. 40, 1905, pp. 481 ff.

[156] See W. H. Jones, *op. cit.*, pp. 303 ff.

[157] See F. E. Kind, *Pauly-Wissowa's Real-Encyclopädie*, vol. 3A:1, 1927, pp. 1119 ff.

[158] Babylonian Berakoth 60b, R. Huna quoting Rab quoting R. Meir.

say, They will perform a miracle for me',[159] 'Ever keep in obscurity and last out'.[160]

Already the Scriptures represent certain behaviour as constantly incumbent on a person. You may have to observe it 'day and night'. This is how the good shepherd watches over his flock[161] and God over his people,[162] and how Nehemiah had the rebuilding of the walls of Jerusalem guarded.[163] Above all, unceasing occupation with the law is enjoined;[164] indeed, you must speak of it 'when you sit, walk, lie down and rise up'.[165] (A terrible prediction of idolatry 'day and night' occurs in Jeremiah.[166]) Other expressions used are 'at all times' and 'continually'. The Psalmist will bless the Lord thus,[167] he extols the man who never deviates from righteousness[168] and he calls on us to persist in seeking God.[169] Wisdom knows that a true friend is unshaken by adversity;[170] it exhorts a husband to stay steadfastly attached to his wife;[171] and it advises you, since all must die, to enjoy yourself and keep on wearing festive robes.[172] Often the meaning is not exactly 'every minute' but rather 'habitually, whenever the appropriate moment arrives'. The judges Moses appointed to relieve him were to take any dispute as it came up,[173] the sacrificial code prescribes the offering of one lamb in the morning and one in the evening in perpetuity.[174]

In the first half of the second century A.D. a special form crops up for the enunciation of duties always to be borne in mind: 'ever' or 'never' (*le'olam* or *le'olam lo'*) should a man do or be so-and-so, or—less common—in direct address, 'ever' or 'never' do or be so-and-so. It is met neither in the Old Testament[175] nor, say, in Sirach

---

[159] Babylonian Taanith 20b, R. Adda bar Ahaba quoting R. Jannai.
[160] Babylonian Sanhedrin 14a, 92a, R. Eleazar ben Pedath.
[161] Genesis 31.39 f.
[162] Isaiah 27.3, Psalms 121.3 f.; cp. Jeremiah 33.25.
[163] Nehemiah 4.3.
[164] Joshua 1.8, Psalms 1.2.
[165] Deuteronomy 6.7.
[166] Jeremiah 16.13.
[167] Psalms 34.2, 40.17; cp. 145.2 'every day'.
[168] Psalms 106.3.
[169] Psalms 105.4, I Chronicles 16.11.
[170] Proverbs 17.17.
[171] Proverbs 5.19.
[172] Ecclesiastes 9.8.
[173] Exodus 18.22.
[174] Exodus 29.38.
[175] Some Biblical provisions do contain the word: 21.6, Leviticus 25.46, Deuteronomy 23.7. But it never opens a law and, moreover, its meaning is

or the Dead Sea texts; nor is it discernible behind the Greek Apocrypha or the New Testament.[176] It is adumbrated in an argument of Joshua ben Hananiah and fully developed by the time of Akiba.

Among its roots must be those cases where with an obligation applicable to a limited area is contrasted one applicable without reservation. Frequently this happens in controversy, one Rabbi advocating a narrower scope, another the ever or never. Where there is a priest, heave-offering is to be given from the best, where there is no priest, simply from that which keeps—but R. Judah holds that 'ever one gives from the best'.[177] According to R. Eliezer, though rain is wanted only from the end of Tabernacles, it should be mentioned in the Eighteen Benedictions from the first day: to mention it, he urges, is not to ask for it. To which R. Joshua replies that, on the basis of this reasoning, 'ever (in summer as well as winter) one would have to mention it'.[178] On the Ninth of Ab one works or abstains from work according to local custom, though the disciples of the Sages abstain everywhere. However, Rabban Simeon ben Gamaliel (father of Judah the Prince) favours universal abstention: 'ever should a man make himself a disciple of the Sages'.[179] This example[180] shows well how these antitheses might help on the growth of the form: the statement just quoted could easily be detached from its original, specific context so as to figure as an independent maxim.

Very likely, a dcisive role in the evolution was played by Stoic influence. That school was thinking a good deal in terms of ever and never, activities and attitudes to be stuck to or shunned with determined consistency; and its diction reflects this bias. The Stoic ideal,

---

somewhat different: it refers to the immutability of the state of affairs ordained, 'for ever' rather than 'ever'. At first sight, I Chronicles 16.15 looks like adumbrating the Rabbinic maxims: 'Remember le'olam his covenant'. Even here, however, the emphasis is on the lastingness of the bond. The verse continues: 'the words he commanded to a thousand generations'. A comparison with Psalms 105.8 confirms this interpretation: here it is God who remembers le'olam, surely, 'for ever'.

[176] If one were to make a Hebrew translation of Tobith 4.19, Luke 18.1, Colossians 4.6, I Thessalonians 4.17, 5.15 ff., one would use 'at all times' and 'continually'.

[177] Mishnah Terumoth 2.4.

[178] Mishnah Taanith 1.1.

[179] Mishnah Pesahim 4.5.

[180] Others: Mishnah Shabbath 16,2, Yoma 4.5, Sukkah 5.8, Ketuboth 5.7, Menahoth 11.2, Negaim 1.4, Parah 4.4, Miqwaoth 8.3.

Cicero explains, is 'to be in accord with virtue ever'.[181] 'Ever in promise', he says, 'attention is to be paid to the meaning, not to the words'.[182] 'There should ever be pondered all human things that may befall a man'.[183] What Marcus Aurelius finds admirable is 'Nothing else to consult even for a moment than reason, ever the same course',[184] and he tells himself, 'Continuously reflect who they are by whom you want to be approved'.[185]

Certainly, one need not be a Stoic to tender emphatically general advice. Cicero himself was not one, strictly. Ever and never may be resorted to by any self-confident instructor. Publilius Syrus counsels: 'By what means you may ensure your safety, ever reflect'.[186] (It is indeed remarkable how rare this phrasing is in his fragments.) Christopher Robin warns his mother: 'You must never go down to the end of the town, Unless you go down with me'. It remains probable that the Stoic mood was a major factor in this matter.

Considering the popularity of the Stoic system throughout the Empire, we can hardly be surprised it should have had an impact on the shaping of Talmudic principles. The range of the form, too, speaks strongly in favour of this thesis: it is distinctly tied to ethics, refined religion, wise living, philosophy. And some additional support is furnished by the fact that the addressee of these precepts is regularly designated by the rather universal noun ʾadham, 'human', 'man'. It appears even where the rule can be meant only for a Jew: 'Ever should a man run to a fulfilment of commandment, and even on a Sabbath' (when, normally, one walks at a leisurely pace).[187] To be sure, this noun is freely employed also in injunctions not couched in this style: 'Nothing is proper for a man on a festival but either eating and drinking or sitting and studying'.[188]

The form proved an enormous success, flourishing throughout the Middle Ages and almost to the present day. Tobit reminds his son: 'Pour out your bread and wine on the tomb of the just'. A

---

[181] Cicero, *De Officiis* 3.3.13.
[182] Cicero, *De Officiis* 1.13.40.
[183] Cicero, *Tusculan Disputations* 3.14.30.
[184] Marcus Aurelius, *Thoughts* 1.8.
[185] Marcus Aurelius, *Thoughts* 7.62.
[186] Publilius Syrus, *Sentences* 520.
[187] Babylonian Berakoth 66, R. Tanhuma quoting R. Joshua ben Levi.
[188] Babylonian Pesahim 68b, Betzah 15b, R. Eliezer.

twelfth-century Jewish translator adds *leʿolam*.[189] For him, such a teaching would not be complete without this particle.

An example of source criticism going astray without the corrective of form criticism is furnished by twelve curses which, according to Deuteronomy, were solemnly laid on twelve crimes as the Israelites entered the promised land.[190] The catalogue has been deemed an omnium gatherum due to the post-Deuteronomic, final redactor R: the offences are culled, it is said, 'not from the Deuteronomic work but from the whole of the Pentateuch'.[191] At first sight, no doubt they do look quite disparate: setting up an image, despising father or mother, removing a landmark, misdirecting the blind, perverting the judgment of the stranger, intercourse with the father's wife, with a beast, with the sister, with the mother-in-law, homicide and sentencing an innocent person to death for a bribe. For the moment, I leave out of account the last imprecation, upon 'him who does not uphold all this law'. By general source-critical considerations, one would readily be led to the conclusion just quoted.

As soon, however, as we reflect on the form, 'Cursed is he who does so-and-so', things appear in a different light. The invocation of divine vengeance is appropriate where, grave as the misdeed is, human justice cannot cope with it; chiefly, that is, because it takes place in secret, or because it is committed by the mighty against the helpless, or because it is of an insidious nature that eludes precise definition. If, with this datum in mind, we go through the list again, it turns out anything but a random, heterogeneous compilation. The first transgression is not just setting up an image but setting it up 'in secret'. The attribute is in the code itself. In the case of the second, contemptuous treatment of a parent, apart from the fact that the victim will often be loath to publicize it, it may be most difficult to pinpoint a concrete wrongdoing.[192] The third, interference with a boundary sign, is invariably perpetrated by stealth. The fourth, exploitation of the blind, not only implies a decided

---

[189] Tobit 4.17. See D. C. Simpson, *The Book of Tobit*, in R. H. Charles, *The Apocrypha and Pseudepigrapha of the Old Testament*, vol. 1, 1913, p. 213.

[190] Deuteronomy 27.15 ff.

[191] See E. F. Kautzsch and A. Bertholet, *Die Heilige Schrift des Alten Testaments*, 4th ed., vol. 1, 1922, p. 309.

[192] On the shame-cultural aspect of this curse, see my lecture in Orita, vol. 3, 1969, pp. 38 f.

superiority on the blackguard's part but also can assume so many devious, treacherous shapes—a misleading hint, a handkerchief displayed à la Iago—that even a modern court might have to give up. (It would, of course, be a gross mistake to confine 'blind' in this text to its literal meaning.) The fifth, oppression of the alien, is similar: strong versus weak, and countless subtle ways of trampling on him. The sixth is not just slaying but slaying 'in secret': again, specified in the code. Then four cases of illicit intercourse—always occurring in private. The same is true of the last crime, of a bribe for a miscarriage of justice; and besides, the judge's powerful position makes earthly retribution unlikely.

The appeal to heaven in these three circumstances—the evil is hidden, done by one who can defy censure or of a kind too vague to be justiciable—is amply documented throughout Scripture, and it plays an enormous part in the laws: 'If a person sins in that he hears a curse pronounced (by the victim of an unsolved crime on doer or abettor), and he is a witness whether he has seen it or known of it but does not tell, he shall bear his iniquity',[193] 'If you afflict a widow or orphan and they cry to me, I shall surely hear their cry'[194] and so forth. No wonder the curse is a prominent instrument of intertribal or international coexistence. In the final covenant between Jacob and Laban, the reason—the absence of effective human guarantees—is spelled out: 'No man is with us', Laban says, 'see, God is witness between me and you'.[195] Paradoxically, the lack of sanction in international affairs constitutes a graver problem today, in the era of UNO, than in those periods of antiquity when God or the gods were held to watch over them.

The spirit of the collection has much in common with that of the Ten Commandments. I incline to a pretty early date. The order of the four sexual sins is noteworthy: father's wife, bestiality, sister, mother-in-law. One would expect the three instances of incest together and bestiality at the end.[196] A possible inference is that the original version of the dooms goes back to before sister and mother-in-law were prohibited, these being subsequently appended to father's wife and beast. It is also arguable, however, that the code is not quite that old and that the strange array results from its drawing

---

[193] Leviticus 5.1, cp. Judges 17.2.
[194] Exodus 22.22.
[195] Genesis 31.50.
[196] See my *Studies in Biblical Law*, 1947, repr. 1969, pp. 77 ff.

on prior legislation: it is that source which grew up in stages, with new taboos tacked on to an existing set instead of being worked in, and the code under discussion does not bother to rationalize the sequence.

A glance at other systems supports my approach. Ancient Greek lists of imprecations cover much the same field as the one in Deuteronomy. Even in Plato, neglect of filial obligations,[197] removal of a landmark[198] and faithlessness to a stranger[199] are still given over to divine chastisement. In commenting on the last-mentioned wrong, Plato, like Laban, explains the need for intervention from on high: 'He is without companions or kinsfolk'. An inscription of Chios[200] goes further, frankly assigning to the curse last place when all worldly remedies have failed. It starts by imposing a fine on misappropriation of public land. It goes on to lay down that if the officials who ought to exact it fail to do so, they themselves are liable. And what if the higher officials who should make them pay are equally remiss? Now we come to the ultimate resort: they are cursed.

Comparison may also supply a clue as to the standing of the twelfth curse which I have so far neglected—threatening 'him who does not uphold all this law'. On the stele of Teos known as the Dirae Teiae,[201] there are a number of warnings with the structure 'Whoever does so-and-so, that man shall perish, he and his house'; and the last two are aimed at a magistrate not properly proclaiming the catalogue and at a person not respecting the stele itself. Imprecations of this and similar kinds are also met in Greece proper. The entire constitution of Solon was protected by a curse—at least Dio says so,[202] enough for my purpose. The twelfth curse, then, may contemplate an attack, in some form or another, on the authority of the norms as such—a crime that certainly belongs to the type to combat which the deity's help is badly wanted.

Perhaps it is worth observing that, if the community in its battle against malefactors turns to the Almighty only as a *pis aller*, it close-

---

[197] Plato, *Laws* 4.717B, 9.880E f.
[198] Plato, *Laws* 8.842E f.
[199] Plato, *Laws* 5.729E f.
[200] 5653 a 20 in H. Collitz and F. Bechtel, *Sammlung griechischer Dialektinschriften*, vol. 3, pt. I, 1905, p. 703.
[201] 5632 in H. Collitz and F. Bechtel, *op. cit.*, pp. 690 ff.
[202] Dio Chrysostomus, *Discourses* 80.6.

ly mirrors individual behaviour. Indeed, whether we fight against or for something, we prefer to rely on *les gros bataillons*. 'God's opportunity', in the words of Scott, 'is man's extremity'. Unquestionably, there lurks here some lack of faith. But, by and large, unless we abdicate responsibility for what little seems to be in our hands, we cannot act very differently. Synagogue preachers like to dwell on Biblical heroes who, in critical situations, both prayed and took all reasonable steps to succeed—say, Jacob when, on his journey home from Laban, he was going to encounter Esau.[203]

By the way, even now, in general people swear (I mean, those who do, none of you, of course) when debarred from effective action. This, to be sure, goes for atheists as well as believers. Yet I wonder—without playing down other factors—whether the primeval role of the curse does not still occupy a little corner in the collective unconscious.

It is contrary to Jewish tradition to end on an ill-omened note,[204] so I must not take my leave of you with curses. Instead, let me remind you that these reflections on legal rules are many of them applicable, *mutatis mutandis*, to rules in other fields, among them the jolly ones of cooking and love-making. A San Franciscan recipe for fondue runs: 'Allow bread crumbs to dry slightly ... toss the cheeses ... stir until smooth'.[205] This is descended in direct line from old-time Wisdom—by which, I should note, I mean not only the Hebrew variety but also the classical one, basically alike: for making Greek wine, Cato in his treatise On Agriculture writes, 'carefully gather ripe grapes, add...a measure of pure salt...',[206] as to truffles, Apicius says, 'boil with leeks'.[207] The sage is addressing his disciple. Here are some contemporary amatory directions: 'Always have a medical examination before you come to any conclusion',[208] 'Pay a lot of attention to the conditions, time, place, lights on or off',[209] 'Hug her but also tell her that you love her. Kiss him but also tell him that you love him'.[210] (The last example might

---

[203] Genesis 32.1 ff.
[204] See J. H. Hertz, *The Pentateuch and Haftorahs*, 1938, p. 970, on the repetition of Malachi 3.23 after 3.25 in the Lesson from the Prophets.
[205] See The Junior League of San Francisco, *San Francisco à la Carte*, 1979, p. 41.
[206] Cato, *On Agriculture* 24.
[207] Apicius, *On Culinary Art* 7.16.5.320.
[208] See H. Fensterheim and J. Baer, *Don't say Yes when you want to say No* (The Assertiveness Training Book), 1975, New Dell edition 1978, repr. 1981, p. 154.
[209] Ibid., p. 155.
[210] Ibid., p. 138.

tempt one to investigate upcoming structures, more or less laboured, resulting from the need for evenhandedness between the two sexes.[211]) Equally deriving from antiquity. A newly deciphered hieroglyphic message by a father to his son reads: 'Do not take liberties with a woman whose husband is listening to your words'.[212] The typical German cookbook prescription of my young days was impersonal, distant and authoritative: *Man nehme zwei Eier*, 'one take two eggs'. I shall not go into its complicated history. Nowadays, the Wisdom infinitive is to the fore: *Den Braten fünf Minuten stehen lassen*, 'to let the roast stand for five minutes'. Even the direct address is gaining ground, but as it is based on the polite *Sie*, 'you', instead of on *du*, 'thou', the tone is not really intimate and paternal.[213] (Another significant change in my lifetime is uniformization: every recipe in a collection is arranged the same way.) From the province of Cupid, there is Nietzsche's *Du gehst zu Frauen? Vergiss die Peitsche nicht!*,[214] 'You are visiting women? Do not forget the whip', or Goethe's much more philogynous rebuttal of the complaint that a woman will flit from one suitor to another: *Tadle sie nicht, sie sucht einen beständigen Mann*,[215] 'Do not blame her, she is looking for a constant man'.

N.B. The very title of the volume containing the advice about medical check-ups, lights on or off etc., shows the Wisdom imperative: 'Don't say Yes when you want to say No'. Such titles are common now in this country. 'Do it yourself' is proverbial. Twelve minutes at Cody's bookshop gave me, from Business, 'Don't bank on it',[216] 'Go for it',[217] 'Make yourself clear';[218] from Health, 'Be slim and healthy',[219] 'Eat your Way to Health',[220] 'Eat right to stay healthy',[221] 'Improve your Sight without Glasses',[222] 'Live your

---

[211] For a special, early case in I Corinthians 7.12 ff., see my lecture in *Jesus and Man's Hope*, ed. D. G. Miller and D. Y. Hadidian, 1971, vol. 2, p. 240.

[212] See L. M. Boyd's *Grab Bag* in *San Francisco Chronicle*, November 1, 1980, p. 29.

[213] See *Brigitte Kochbuch*, 1970, p. 18.

[214] *Also sprach Zarathustra*, Part 1, *Vom alten und jungen Weiblein* i.f.

[215] *Goethes Gespräche*, ed. F. v. Biedermann, rev. W. Herwig, 1965, vol. 1, p. 343.

[216] By M. J. Meyer, 1979.
[217] By M. Douglas, 1979.
[218] By J. O. Morris, 1980.
[219] By L. Clark, 1972.
[220] By I. B. Holbrook, 1972.
[221] By D. Burkitt, 1979.
[222] By Editorial Committee of *Science of Life Books*, 10th ed., 1975.

Health',[223] 'Run to Health'.[224] Particularly interesting is 'Heal yourself with Vegetables, Fruits and Grains',[225] a translation: the French original carries the old-fashioned designation 'Treatment of Diseases by Vegetables, Fruits and Grains'. A seachange on the voyage to the States—though Europe will doubtless catch up before long. Finally, from Psychology, 'Don't push the River',[226] 'Get your Message across',[227] 'If you meet the Buddha on the Road, kill him',[228] 'Own your own Life',[229] 'Spare the Couch',[230] 'Stand up! Speak out! Talk back!',[231] 'Stop running scared'.[232] We have to do with a new-established style of title. It is not found, say, in Freud, Jung or even their immediate disciples over here; nor, when I went from Cody's to the store in the Students' Union where they sell books recommended for courses, did I notice a single specimen—so the chief priests have not yet taken to it. It is a concomitant of a peculiar outgrowth of the—au fond marvellous—American zest for experimentation: the reign of gurus who, each with his novel tao to salvation, guide us through the twenty-four hours of the day.

Not by chance it comes hard on the heels of a proliferation of 'How to' tracts. 'How to' also has its pedigree, going back to the ancient manuals of crafts. Cato heads a paragraph 'how (*quomodo*) one should construct a mill',[233] another one 'how one should preserve lentils'.[234] The large-scale use of the phrase for entitling whole books implies an immense popularization of technology. Our magi instruct us in the fixing of anything whatever. But whereas at the 'How to' stage, we are still allowed to choose our needs, the imperativists-imperialists—'Do', 'Do not'—determine these as well as the answers.

This bent explains why the Wisdom imperative in titles frequently shades off into the imperative that expresses a detailed order.

---

[223] By R. and J. Halpern, 1980.
[224] By P. D. Wood, 1980.
[225] Translation by H. Stern-Montagny, 1976, of J. Valnet, *Traitement des Maladies par les Légumes, les Fruits et les Céréales*.
[226] By B. Stevens, 1970.
[227] By J. R. Diekman, 1979.
[228] By S. B. Kopp, 1972.
[229] By R. G. Abell with C. W. Abell, 1976.
[230] By D. L. Tasto and E. W. Skje, 1979.
[231] By R. E. Alberti and M. Emmons, 1975.
[232] By H. Fensterheim and J. Baer, 1977.
[233] Cato, *On Agriculture* 19.1.
[234] Cato, *On Agriculture* 116.

'Don't push the River' is still in the nature of a general, profound rule. 'Stand up! Speak out! Talk back!' is only partially that; it at least half conjures up the specific occasion on which these directions have to be barked out. Nor is the affinity with advertising slogans accidental. A report on Fat Profits in Diet Aids quotes 'Slim down fast without going hungry', 'Take weight off and keep it off' and so forth.[235] You are being offered the infallible remedy: there is no excuse for not buying it. Education gives way to dictate, strategy to tactics, and the groves of academe are being turned into workshop or drillground.

I started researching into patterns of love advice in the early fifties, during my period at Aberdeen. The University Library there kept all Erotica locked away in a sort of poison section and even professors had to specially ask for any item they wanted. I have done a few brave things in my life but, believe me, none of them compares to facing the North of Scotland lady at the desk and requesting a copy of the Kamasutra. For that, I feel, I deserve the Victoria Cross.

---

[235] In *San Francisco Chronicle*, November 3, 1980, p. 28.

EXCURSUS 1 TO LECTURE III

'The form of a statement may reveal a good deal, apart from its content'. If it is oral, this goes even for intonation, a gesture, a twinkle.

I remember, in my Cambridge days, showing a 'gremial' generously helpful to refugees the draft of a lecture which contained a remark I did not mean seriously. I forget what it was, say, 'a Roman politician did not lie to his constituency'. He boggled at it and when I replied that the class would get me from my manner, also from their by then pretty fair acquaintance with my philosophy and, at a pinch, if they did not, I would sense it and add a quick supplement, he declared that the text by itself ought to convey the intended sense, with no assistance whatever from inflexion, personal ties, interaction and the like. Indeed, by and by I learned that even the text itself had preferably be understated. His was a Wykehamist attitude: the classical restraint of an English gentleman extolled, for example, in André Maurois's *Les Silences du Colonel Bramble*. As a teacher, he never procured his flock a 'high' and he never let them down—he was dependable and slightly boring. My use of extrinsic aids springs from a far greater, vulgar involvement; and while I frequently manage to carry my public along, now and then, for some reason or other, I fail dismally.

Perhaps the champions of austerity will be less disapproving if reminded of support for me in antiquity. Demosthenes considered declamation the foremost branch of oratory,[1] Aristotle complained about the lack of treatises on the subject,[2] his disciple Theophrastus, taking it up, compared speaker and actor[3] and Cicero coined the phrase 'eloquence of the body'.[4] It is not, by the way, as if the purists were not acting. Only their object is not to drive home their specific points—that is the need of those who have not yet arrived—but to convey an overall impression of security, impartiality, distance, standing above it. 'Dumb, we shout', says

---

[1] Philodemus, *On Rhetoric* 1.196.3, Cicero, *Brutus* 38.142, *Orator* 17.56, and others.
[2] Aristotle, *The Art of Rhetoric* 3.1.3.
[3] Cicero, *De Oratore* 3.59.221.
[4] Cicero, *Orator* 17.55.

an old proverb;[5] 'immobile, we run' it might continue. (A parallel can now be found over here: many a guru, a picture of impassivity and disinterestedness, is making it fast.) I grant that their toning down of presentation educates their listeners to spot irony more readily than do continental or Americans ones. The latter just do not expect it when confronted by a dead-pan face. Economy breeds subtlety.

Of course, there are gradations within the two camps. Reticence in Britain is required more strictly in the academic field than in some others, the political, for instance. 'While the speech for the Gregorian Calendar by Lord Macclesfield, a consummate astronomer, was received with yawns, that of Lord Chesterfield who, as he himself tells us, was utterly ignorant of the science, but a captivating orator, chained the attention and won the votes of the House'.[6] In the Germany of my youth, though in general rules were less rigid, much contempt was felt for unassimilated Jews on the ground of 'talking with the hands', *mit den Händen reden*. Personal characteristics, too, come into play. My friendly instructor was uncommonly correct, I—from day one bent on outshining my elder brother—am avid for applause.

English protest against the overrating of frills—not the same as outright rejection—started early. Bacon comments on Demosthenes's view:[7] 'A strange thing that that part of an Orator which is but superficial, and rather the virtue of a Player, should be placed so high'. Even on the stage, he notes, originally, the quality of acting was of little moment: the earliest authors of tragedies performed themselves and did not call in professional actors. What, then, brought about the imbalance? The stupidity of the mass who goes for glitter: 'There is in human Nature generally more of the fool than of the wise'. This elitism would become the hallmark of the British public school. Actually, staying with the bare text wards off not only the rabble within the borders but foreigners as well. Already the ancient masters perceived the relevance of the problem to retention or bridging of both class and national divisions. 'Anything pertaining to delivery', says Cicero,[8] 'conveys a certain

---

[5] *Dum tacent clamant.*
[6] See W. Mathews, *The Great Conversers*, 1878, p. 206.
[7] Bacon, *Essays, Of Boldness* init., cited by Cope, *The Rhetoric of Aristotle*, ed. Sandys, 1877, vol. 3, p. 4.
[8] Cicero, *De Oratore* 3.59.223.

meaning naturally. For this reason, the ignorant, the crowd and indeed the barbarians are most moved by it. For words move only one who is conjoined in a society of a common language...Delivery, carrying the mind's emotion to the outside, moves all since the minds of all are stirred by the same emotions and it is by the same signs that they recognize them in others and manifest them themselves'. Clearly, renunciation of non-verbal, 'natural' relish ties in with insularity.

Maybe it can come about only in a highly masculine culture. In a previous publication,[9] I quoted Oscar Wide to the effect that, in conversation with women, you should listen less to what they say than to how they say it. This, *au fond*, is to concede that, less unilinear that men, they will not be confined to one narrow channel of communication. To be sure, what prompted the quip was pure machismo: at the time, feminine fluidity counted as sweet, childlike, a bit treacherous, well below male earnestness. In the same book,[10] I complained that most writers on Roman law were leaving the study of form to the professors of literature and poetry—possibly a result of the same male inflexibility.

Where I go wrong is in transferring what belongs in a live show to the printed page. Often when I write I feel as if talking. As a result, trusting to an imaginary contact, I may express myself in a fashion apt to mislead even a sophisticated reader. Quintilian observes that an audience will detect sarcasm by heeding one or more of three clues: modulation, character of the orator, the statement as such.[11] Whereas my Camford mentors would keep to *rei natura* even in speech, I am apt to rely on *pronuntiatio* and *persona* even in writing. Exactly where the line ought to be drawn is not easy to determine. Here are a few instances.

A recent number of the California Law Review celebrated the start of the Jurisprudence and Society Program at Boalt Hall. For people overseas I should explain that university law journals in the States are directed by students who may thoroughly revise a contribution; so I collaborated only on being assured by Dean Kadish that he would keep an eye on things and that no changes would be made without my consent. My article introduced Sophocles as

---

[9] *Forms of Roman Legislation*, p. 6.
[10] *Op. cit.*, p. 1.
[11] Quintilian, *Institutio Oratoria* 8.6.54.

originator of the detective story.[12] I concluded by saying that I would not now discuss the two millennia between him and the modern whodunnit but—last sentence in my draft: 'Hopefully, I reserve this study for the silver jubilee of J.S.P.'. Attached to 'hopefully' was a footnote: 'Student editors, please note that this is the approved manner of using the adverb'. I am sure that, had I been conversing with them, or even had they been pupils of mine and therefore known me well enough, they would have realized that I was inviting them to laugh together with me at the pedantic, repetitious criticism of the extended application that has long gained currency. However, as it was, they thought that I was truly concerned about this grammatical issue and, worse, I doubted their grasp of it. They were seconded by the Dean, otherwise very protective of my idiosyncracies. Evidently, I had failed to link up properly and I rephrased the ending.

In a forthcoming tract on New Testament ethics I write: 'There is indeed a blend of shame and guilt mechanism in each civilisation and each individual (except for California where we do without either)—not to mention the fact that a deep enough probing would reveal an intrinsic overlap of the two emotions'. John Noonan, whom I asked for his comments, is put off by the inconsistency with another passage where I point out that, in Luke,[13] the invitees to the Great Supper keep up appearances, 'tendering apologies that would go down well in the Berkeley hills—I just married, I have arranged to inspect some real estate I bought' etc. I do not think I shall make any change. I cannot believe there will be many who do not see that the aside in brackets is to be taken with a grain of salt.

In the following case, he does catch me out treating the written word as if spoken. I draw attention to a split among the Rabbis between purists, with absolute standards, and realists, taking account of period and milieu. According to the latter, far less is to be required of Noah, living in a godless age, than of Moses or David. I add: 'Conduct barely so-so under Carter may be splendid under Nixon'. John Noonan urges that the contrast between the two administrations is no longer so sharp as it once seemed. I fully agree with him.[14] In fact, I find Carter's exploitation of his rebirth for the

---

[12] *California Law Review*, vol. 68, 1980, pp. 301 ff. An expanded German translation will come out as a *Konstanzer Universitätsrede* shortly.
[13] Luke 14.16 ff., as contrasted with Matthew 22.1 ff.
[14] Written prior to Billygate.

purpose of advancement particularly distasteful. (Though a realist will be aware that, in a Southerner, it is not quite so calculated as it would be in others.) In a lecture, my voice would do all that is needed. Without it, it is only the rise from censorious 'barely so-so' to enthusiastic 'splendid' that signals tongue-in-cheek—and that is probably too little.

Lastly, describing in a paper on Josephus[15] the court-Jew professor in Europe, I maintain that, while not fully accepted by the gentile colleagues, he is also distrusted by his correligionists: they are conscious that 'we are hand in glove with the establishment, careful not to let the inferior contacts intrude overmuch'. Helen warns me that few American readers will apprehend the ironical thrust of 'the inferior contacts'. What I mean is not that Moses Cohen the peddler is in fact less worthy or interesting than Moses Cohen the mathematician or historian but that, in parts of the world, such is the verdict of the arrogant, hidebound ruling set; hence whoever craves there a position of eminence must compromise with prejudice, must not flaunt too much his intimacy with those looked down on. In England, I assume, I shall be understood, in the States, with a higher degree of literal-mindedness, maybe I shall not. Why did I not make myself clearer by recourse to inverted commas: 'careful not to let the "inferior" contacts intrude overmuch'? In general, if you have to announce 'here comes irony', I feel it is not worth having. It is possible, however, that my disinclination to this crutch goes back to an attack on underlining I heard in the 1920s from a teacher at my Gymnasium, Ernst Ochs, who could compete with my Cantabrigian mystagogue: *Das Unterstreichen ist das pöbelhafte Kind des parlamentarischen Zeitalters*, 'Underlining is the plebeian child of the parliamentary age'.

Rather to my surprise, I discover that the original German version of this piece is quite straightforward, with *Brüder*, 'brothers', instead of 'inferior contacts'; all the more striking as it was an address to the Bavarian Academy,[16] and as I explained above, it is easier to be ironical in oral communication. Apparently, in my native country, the subject was too loaded for both my audience and me to allow of any *exornatio*, elegant roundabout.

---

[15] *Journal of Jewish Studies*, vol. 31, 1980, p. 34.
[16] *Typologie im Werk des Flavius Josephus*, Bayerische Akademie der Wissenschaften, Phil.-Hist. Klasse, Sitzungsberichte 1977, no. 6, p. 26.

Who knows?—my overdoing it may betray various instincts bearing on power and weakness: to play, to tease, to test, to attract at once and make things difficult, to wield a secret weapon, to entrap, to outwit, to be chased (by friend or foe), to remain in the twilight, to escape full responsibility. In close relationships, Helen insists, irony—*dissimulatio* in Latin—is often a distancing rather than a positive force. She has Plato on her side[17] (also Rilke[18]): his Alcibiades is lyrical about the great moment when he broke through to the true Socrates, who for once dispensed with his habitual deviousness. What made him eager for that miracle in the first place?

---

[17] *Symposium* 216 E.
[18] See the quotations in R. Bly, *Selected Poems of Rainer Maria Rilke*, 1979, p. 188.

EXCURSUS 2 TO LECTURE III

In the Ten Commandments, 'God's voice compels the individual conscience'. My friend William David Davies, whom I asked to vet parts of the typescript, suggested I substitute 'accountability' for 'conscience', seeing that the latter word—Latin *conscientia*, from Greek *syneidos* or *syneidesis*—is missing from the Old Testament. He has contributed the authoritative article on it to the Interpreter's Dictionary of the Bible.[1]

I was aware, when writing, of what modern theologians make of its absence, but I do not go along with them. I explained my standpoint to William David, and he encouraged me to set it down. Here, then, is what I feel.

Let me start with *tu quoque*: they talk freely about Mosaic 'morality', 'religion', etc., with no better textual backing. I wonder what the Hebrew for 'accountability' may be.

Next, what is meant by saying that a term does occur? In many cases, such as 'husband' for *baʿal* or *ʾish*, 'covenant' for *berith*, 'to create' for *qana*, the remoteness of the translation from the original is obvious at a glance. Some measure of discrepancy, however, is always there: not a single Hebrew-English pair is truly alike. The only solution—even it by no means perfect—would be to publish in ancient Hebrew.

In a less quibbling spirit—though absence of a term often betokens absence of the thing, this is far from inevitable. The sources contain no equivalent of 'nuclear power': it was not invented. On the other hand, parents taught children long before there were the verbs 'to instruct'—let alone the nouns 'teaching', 'instruction'[2]—and people behaved responsibly or recklessly about spears and fires long before 'due care' and 'negligence' made their debut. Psalmists and prophets structured their utterances by means of *parallelismus membrorum*, but the device was christened only by an Oxford professor of the eighteenth century.

There is a further factor of enormous importance: not seldom the late birth or adoption of a word is due to the previous self-

---

[1] Vol. 4, 1962, pp. 671 ff.
[2] On the posteriority of the action noun, see my *Roman Law*, 1969, pp. 11 ff.

understoodness of what it expresses.³ At this moment, in English, while we do have 'vegetarian', we are without a settled label for the less gentle feeder—not because he does not exist but, on the contrary, because he is taken for granted. Common occurrence, that is, may join non-occurrence in being left unnamed. No doubt, we could easily fill the gap; and should current nutrition fads prevail, 'meat-and-fish-eater' or 'non-vegetarian' will become part of established usage, or perhaps 'carnivore' will be extended from the animal world to the human. But the priority of 'vegetarian' will remain. Molière's *bourgeois*, before losing his naivety as he trains for the status of *gentilhomme*, has no inkling that he is an author of 'prose'—*prorsa oratio*, 'straight speech'.

The point is that words are coined to designate the striking, not the ordinary; and the striking is often the less frequent, in fact, it may be striking precisely because it is exceptional. I got interested in the phenomenon years ago, when dealing with *intestatus*, 'intestate', in the XII Tables of fifth-century B.C. Rome. Scholars were then agreed that, as Latin had only a negative term for a person leaving no will, this figure must have been rare. That seemed to me fantastic: testacy the norm as early as that, and among the have-nots as well as the haves! The correct conclusion is just the opposite. Primeval Latin had no appellation for a person who allowed his estate to go to the law-appointed heirs: everybody did that. It was for the novel, remarkable step of willmaking that a verb was introduced, *testari*. Hence, when the XII Tables wished to say something about the old and still by far most usual way, they had to resort to a negative, *intestatus*. Similarly, *experiri*, 'to try out', *auspicari*, 'to take auspices', draw attention to actions which, to begin with at least, are special. There are no verbs for the unexciting conditions without a try out, without auspices. So the doer of the special can be described by a positive past participle, *expertus*, *auspicatus*, but the abstainer, who represents the rule, only by negativing this: *inexpertus*, *inauspicatus*. A passage from King David's dirge about Saul and Jonathan is instructive.⁴ 'Tell it not in Gath, lest the daughters of the uncircumcised triumph'. For the

---

³ See my articles in *Revue Historique de Droit Français et Etranger*, ser. 4, vol. 15, 1936, pp. 341 ff., *Tulane Law Review*, vol. 39, 1965, pp. 254 ff., and *Zeitschrift der Savigny-Stiftung*, vol. 90, 1973, Rom. Abt., p. 1 (Engl. version in *Juridical Review*, vol. 85, n.s. 18, 1973, p. 126).

⁴ II Samuel 1.20.

authors of the King James version, 'to circumcise' denotes an outlandish measure. Accordingly, in referring to the standard, not endowed with a tag of its own, they make do with the negative 'uncircumcised'. By contrast, the Hebrews, by the time of this poem, are taken aback by lack of their rite. In the original, therefore, we find a positive adjective, ʿarelim, 'those with foreskin'. To be sure, squeamishness, too, may have inclined the King James team towards the less direct.

The Greeks never spoke of a *polytheos*, 'polytheist'. Yet the predicate is listed in Greek dictionaries. Philo, Jewish outsider, made it up. In modern vocabulary *athéisme* and *polythéisme*, French precursors of 'atheism' and 'polytheism', preceded *monothéisme*. Sixteenth-centutry *athée* (Rabelais) was never followed by *monothée*, and *monothéiste* had to wait for *monothéisme*, seventeenth century. *Déisme* is as late as 1660 (Pascal). Both in French and in English, 'bigamy' and 'polygamy' considerably antedate 'monogamy'.

No woman in the Pentateuch is said to 'love' a parent, suitor, husband or child except Rebeccah who puts one son above the other.[5] A fully developed noun 'love' is not met in this corpus at all. In Fiddler on the Roof,[6] Tevye asks his wife of many years whether she 'loves' him. She finds the question awkward: at their stage, it is inane to bring up, play with, what throughout has been preserved in safekeeping, sacred, central. By putting it, the hero shows himself slightly infected, *angekränkelt*, by the present tendency to cover over insecurity and brittleness with romantic declamation. 'Tell him that you love him'.[7] After all, the show must appeal to a contemporary audience. (I hope somebody has examined, or will examine, the numerous intriguing deviations from Sholem Aleichem.[8]) Though my parents were often at loggerheads, I do not think my father ever needed this kind of reassurance. His son sympathizes with Tevye.

When I lived in England, again and again the German *Schadenfreude*, with no close English parallel, was quoted to me as proving a peculiar German defect. On such occasions, if I was in a bad mood,

---

[5] Genesis 25.28. Cp. Genesis 29.18, 30, 32, 37.3 f., 44.20, Deuteronomy 10.15, 21.15 f.
[6] J. Stein, 1964, pp. 80 ff.
[7] See H. Fensterheim and J. Baer cited above, p. 113.
[8] Hodel's engagement which, in the musical, triggers the question, is found in his *The Old Country*, 1946, pp. 382 ff.

I retorted that it is superfluous to note that which, literally, 'goes without saying': so it was the English who lost. And I was only half-joking. (Among South-German Jewry at least, *neqama*—pronounced *neqome*—the Biblical 'vengeance', came very near *Schadenfreude* with, however, slight differences in application.)

We must not, of course, simplify. The everyday nature of a thing is far from the only feature delaying a title, unusualness far from the only feature promoting it. Again, what is thoroughly familiar in one context may be astounding in another; and perhaps, in the course of millennia, most things have astounded sufficiently to be marked out: 'friend' and 'foe', 'sickness' and 'health', 'to eat' and 'to fast', 'honest' and fraudulent'. Most things—but by no means all. To 'vegetarian', already mentioned, I could add many more examples. There are, as yet, no opposite numbers to 'murderer', 'arsonist', 'cannibal'. 'Straight' has only recently become available, at San Francisco, as a—faintly pejorative—antonym of 'gay'.

Basically, language gives an inverted reflection of reality. It is a laughing mirror in which the small appears large and the large small. The Pythagoreans were on to something when they held[9] that we do not notice the music of the spheres because it is with us right from birth; we are like a coppersmith who becomes indifferent to the din around him; and we hear only the petty interruptions. It is moving that, notwithstanding the comparison with a factory, they assumed those galactic sounds to be of marvellous beauty.

Conscience in the Old Testament. What, for instance, about David's charitableness after all who stood in his way are routed? 'Is there yet any left of the house of Saul, that I may show him kindness for Jonathan's sake?'[10] But, one might object, it is not openly stated that this motive plays a part; we have to infer it. What, then, about two episodes from the Joseph cycle? One for conscience after a misdeed: his brothers, unaware that he is the high Egyptian official who keeps one of them back as hostage, remember what they did to him long ago.[11] 'And they said one to another, We are verily guilty concerning our brother, in that we saw the anguish of his soul; therefore is this distress come upon us'. The other for conscience when tempted: Joseph, purchased by an Egyptian grandee who

---

[9] Aristotle, *On the Heavens* 193.
[10] II Samuel 9.1.
[11] Genesis 42.21.

promotes him to majordomo, is urged by his master's wife to be her paramour.[12] 'But he refused: Behold, my master keeps no watch over me[13] as to what goes on in his house and all that he has he has put into my hand; he is not greater in this house than I; neither has he kept back anything from me but you, because you are his wife. How then can I do this great evil and sin against God?' Or an illustration of a good conscience:[14] the King of Gerar who takes Sarah into his harem, having been given to understand by her as well as Abraham that she is the latter's sister only, is threatened by God with death for appropriating another man's wife, but bravely pleads: 'Will you slay even a righteous nation? Did he not himself say to me, She is my sister, and did she, even she herself, not say, He is my brother? In the simplicity of my heart and the innocency of my hands I done this'. It is hard to believe that a culture possessing the word 'conscience' would have to reformulate these narratives.

At this juncture, I should like to raise a problem not discussed in the literature I have looked up: how come that Greek, in picking a term, so concentrates on the rational, on knowledge? As has long been seen, the verb *synoida*, 'to know together with', originally refers to the sharing of knowledge with somebody else—which has nothing to do with conscience. Hebrew has the same notion, *yadha‘ ’eth*. Joseph's remark which, above (in order to avoid confusion) I rendered 'my master keeps no watch over me as to what goes on in his house', literally signifies: 'my master does not know together with me' and so on. Already two verses before, we are told that his master 'left all he had in Joseph's hand and he knew nothing together with him save the bread which he ate', i.e. save what his trusted servant actually provided him with. You can, however, also share knowledge with yourself: say, you attained it on your own or you are alone in having it. This still is not conscience. But from the fifth century B.C. on, *synoida* and its nouns become fashionable where you share knowledge with yourself in the sense of judging yourself according as you do or do not commit a wrong. Whence this tie-up of self-evaluation with awareness?

Before attempting an answer, I would point out that it very soon loses in strength. Certainly, today, it is quite gone. What we mean

---

[12] Genesis 39.8 f.
[13] On the phrasing in the original, see below, on this page.
[14] Genesis 20.4 f. See above, pp. 51 f., 57 f.

by 'conscience' is no inner knowing but almost an instinct, a moral sense related to guilt. The same is true of German *Gewissen*. If only on this ground, it would be futile to avoid the word in connection with the Old Testament. Today, to recapture something of its pristine application, one would have to turn to 'consciousness'. But I cannot here go into the similarities and dissimilarities between our 'consciousness' movement and ancient doctrines. Historically, the speed with which the rational element gives way to feeling in the Greek suggests that the emphasis on the former must be due to a distinct fifth-century cause.

That period is indeed eminently philosophical. But, more specifically, the key to virtue is widely supposed to lie in information, successful schooling, learning properly taken in.[15] It is quite likely this theory which chiefly leads to the identification of self-judgment with 'the sharing of knowledge with oneself'. Just conceivably, at its inception, the term is favoured by the opponents of Socrates's teaching[16] that no one transgresses wittingly: he errs, they suggest, a person's choice of right or wrong is the very point of his insight. After all, the earliest extant evidence for *syneidesis* is Democritus, whom Plato resents so much that he never once mentions him (as Nixon never mentioned McGovern when they were running against one another). According to Xenophon-Hermogenes,[17] Socrates after his trial uses the verb *synoida*: whereas he can be high-spirited, he says, those participating in the false witness against him must 'share knowledge with themselves' of their wicked conduct. No doubt conscience may be involved, but partly at least the phrase here seems to stress secrecy: privately, those fellows are perfectly acquainted with the truth despite their lies in public. It would still be open to Socrates to argue that even in thus lying they proved their ignorance.

To come back to the Old Testament, there are adumbrations of the Greek semantic evolution though, not surprisingly, adumbrations only. I conclude by giving an example. The Second Book of Samuel records that, as King David looks like being ousted by his son Absalom, a relative of Saul's by name of Shimei insults and curses him. After Absalom's defeat, he asks to be pardoned: 'Your

---

[15] See R. Maschke, *Die Willenslehre im Griechischen Recht*, 1926, pp. 116 ff.
[16] See above, pp. 64 ff.
[17] Xenophon, *Apology* 24.

servant knows that I have sinned'.[18] Not simply 'I have sinned' but 'I know that I have done so'. In fact, the subjective aspect is stressed even further. The Hebrew reads not just *ḥaṭaʾthi*, 'I have sinned', but *ʾani ḥaṭaʾthi*, 'I, even I' or 'I myself have sinned'.

A freak formulation? Impossible. For though David accedes to the plea, the story continues in the First Book of Kings, when Solomon, mindful of a deathbed wish of his father, finds a pretext under which to have Shimei executed; and what he says to him is, 'You know all the evil that your heart knows that you did to my father David'.[19] Awareness is here accented to a remarkable degree. More than that: 'to know the evil that one's heart knows' is highly reminiscent of 'to share knowledge with oneself of an evil'. It would not be wildly off to render: 'Your conscience tells you how you offended'. Commentators have overlooked the motif common to the two portions of the narrative in Samuel and Kings. Some postulate tautology in the latter and cut out 'that your heart knows'. Others interpret the clause as meaning 'of which you are secretly conscious'.[20] But while conscience may dwell on the private (as in the Xenophon text just presented), it need not do so. In this case, it definitely does not. Nothing could be more open than Shimei's confession as he pleads for mercy: 'Let not my Lord remember that which your servant did perversely that day...Your servant knows that I have sinned'. We ought to admit the beginning of something Greek-like here. What accounts for it I have no idea. All I can say is that the entire business of Shimei is full of deep reflection and subtlety.[21]

---

[18] II Samuel 19.21.
[19] I Kings 2.44.
[20] See J. Gray, *I and II Kings*, 1963, p. 108.
[21] On one phase of it, see my article in *Tulane Law Review*, vol. 46, 1972, pp. 653 ff.